GIFTED GAMES™

GIFTED AND TALENTED TEST PREPARATION
for children in preschool and kindergarten

Gateway Gifted Resources™
www.GatewayGifted.com

Thank you for selecting this book. We are a family-owned publishing company - a consortium of educators, book designers, illustrators, parents, and kid-testers.

We would be thrilled if you left us a quick review on the website where you purchased this book!

The Gateway Gifted Resources™ Team
www.GatewayGifted.com

TABLE OF CONTENTS

INTRODUCTION

ABOUT THIS BOOK

This book introduces reasoning exercises, problem-solving tasks, and cognitive skill-building activities to young children through kid-friendly subjects, all in a format designed to help prepare them for taking standardized, multiple-choice gifted and talented assessment tests.

Not only is this book meant to help prepare children for the OLSAT®, COGAT®, and NNAT2®/ NNAT3®, these critical thinking and logic-based materials may also be used as general academic support as well as for other gifted test prep.

THIS BOOK HAS 5 PARTS:

1. Introduction (p. 4-9): About This Book, About Gifted Tests, Test-Taking Tips, the "Gifted Detective Agency"

2. Gifted Workbook (p. 10-49)
- This workbook offers fun, kid-friendly themes to engage children and introduce them to standardized gifted test formats.
- The exercises are meant to be done together with no time limit.
- Each of the sections begins with an easier example task in order to build confidence.
- At the beginning of the sections, be sure to read the information providing explanations and tips.

The "Gifted Detective Agency"
To increase child engagement and to add an incentive to complete book exercises, a detective theme accompanies this book. Read page 9 (the "Gifted Detective Agency") together with your child. The book's characters belong to a detective agency. They want your child to help them solve "puzzles" (the exercises in the book) so that your child can join the detective agency, too! As your child completes the book, allow him/her to "check" the boxes at the bottom of the page. If your child "checks all the boxes," (s)he will "join" the Gifted Detective Agency. We have included boxes at the bottom of every page of the book that features exercises. However, feel free to modify as you see fit the number of pages/exercises your child must complete in order to receive his/her certificate. (The certificate for you to complete with your child's name is on page 102.)

3. Practice Question Sets (p. 51-92)
There are three Practice Question Sets:
- NNAT2®/ NNAT3® Practice Question Set (p. 51)
- COGAT® Practice Question Set (p. 62)
- OLSAT® Practice Question Set (p. 80)

The Practice Question Sets provide:
- an introduction for children to test-taking in a relaxed manner, where parents can provide guidance if needed (without telling the answers!)
- an opportunity for children to practice focusing on a group of questions for a longer time period (something to which most children are not accustomed)
- a way for parents to identify points of strength and weakness in various types of test questions

The Practice Question Sets are meant to help children develop critical thinking and test-taking skills. A "score" (a percentile rank) cannot be obtained from the Practice Question Sets. (See page 6 for more on gifted test scoring.)

Many sections of the three tests' Practice Question Sets can be used interchangeably. For example, if your child will take the OLSAT®, there are sections in both the COGAT® and NNAT2®/ NNAT3® Sets you should use for additional practice. The individual test sections on pages 6-7 include a listing by page number of similar sections among the three tests.

If your child is not taking a particular test, use the Practice Question Sets for additional critical thinking exercises.

4. Directions and Answer Keys (p. 93-101) (Please use a pair of scissors to cut out pages 93-101.)
These pages provide answer keys for both the Workbook and the Practice Question Sets. They also include the directions to read to your child for the Practice Question Sets. (To mimic actual tests, the directions are separate from the child's pages in the Practice Question Sets.)

5. Afterword (p. 102): Information on additional books, free 40+ practice questions, and your child's certificate

A NOTE ON FILLING IN "BUBBLES"
Your child may or may not have to fill in "bubbles" (the circles) to indicate answer choices. When taking a standardized gifted test, if your child is at the Pre-K level, (s)he will most likely only have to point to the answer choice. If your child is at the Kindergarten level, (s)he may have to fill in bubbles. Check with your testing site regarding their "bubble" use.

If your child is at the Kindergarten level, show him/her the "bubbles" under the answer choices. Show your child how to fill in the bubble to indicate his/her answer choice. If your child needs to change his/her answer, (s)he should erase the original mark and fill in the new choice.

A NOTE ON THE QUESTIONS
Because each child has different cognitive abilities, the questions in this book are at varied skill levels. The exercises may or may not require a great deal of parental guidance to complete, depending on your child's ability.

You will notice that most sections of the Workbook begin with a relatively easy question. We suggest always completing at least the first question (which will most likely be an easy one) with him/her. Make sure there is not any confusion about what the question asks or the directions.

WHAT YOU NEED
- *Gifted Games* book
- Answer Keys/Directions (pages 93-101) cut out and by your side
- Pencil and eraser for your child

ABOUT GIFTED TESTS

Gifted tests like those covered in this book assess a child's cognitive abilities, reasoning skills, and problem-solving aptitude.

Testing procedures vary by school and/or program. These tests may be given individually or in a group environment, by a teacher or other testing examiner. These tests may be used as the single determinant for admission to a selective kindergarten or to a school's gifted program. However, some schools/programs use these tests in combination with individual IQ tests administered by psychologists or as part of a student "portfolio." Other schools use them together with tests like Iowa Assessments™ to measure academic achievement. In other instances, schools/programs may use only certain sections of the tests to screen. (See below for more information on the tests' sections.) **Check with your testing site to determine their specific testing procedures.**

Here is a general summary of the scoring process for multiple-choice standardized gifted tests. **Please check with your school/program for its specific scoring and admissions requirements.** First, your child's raw score is established. The raw score equals the number of questions your daughter/son correctly answered. Points are not deducted for questions answered incorrectly. Next, this score is compared to other test-takers of his/her same age group (and, for the COGAT®, the same grade level) using various indices to then calculate your child's percentile rank. If your child achieved the percentile rank of 98%, then (s)he scored as well as or better than 98% of test-takers in his/her age group. In general, most gifted programs only accept top performers of *at least* 98% or *higher*. (Please note that a percentile rank "score" cannot be obtained from our practice material. This material has not been given to a large enough sample of test-takers to develop any kind of base score necessary for percentile rank calculations.)

- **NNAT2® LEVEL A & NNAT3® LEVEL A (NAGLIERI NONVERBAL ABILITY TEST®)**

The NNAT2® Level A and NNAT3® Level A are for Kindergarten. The two tests have a similar design: both contain 48 questions and last approximately 30 minutes. Questions consist of shapes, patterns, and figures. As a "non-verbal" test, the NNAT® doesn't require test-takers to listen to multiple question prompts, nor does it assess verbal comprehension or verbal skills. If unsure which version of the NNAT® your child will take (the NNAT2® or the NNAT3®), please check with your testing site.

The NNAT2®/ NNAT3® Practice Question Set (p. 51) is organized by the two question types of the test: Pattern Completion and Reasoning by Analogy. We suggest referencing the two question type labels listed on page 94 in the Answer Key in order to gain a better understanding of the material in each question type AND to evaluate your child's points of strength and weakness.

You should also use pages 72-75 of the COGAT® Practice Question Set and pages 87, 88, 90 and 92 of the OLSAT® Practice Question Set for additional practice, as these sections deal with shapes/figures.

- **COGAT® (COGNITIVE ABILITIES TEST®) LEVEL 5/6**

The COGAT® Level 5/6 is for Kindergarten. It has 118 questions. The test, about two-hours in length, is administered in different testing sessions. (Children are not expected to complete 118 questions in one session.) Check with your school regarding which level your child will take and for specific test procedures.

The COGAT® measures reasoning skills through exercises including: object classification, identification of similarities/differences, recognizing relationships, analogy completion, sequence completion, pattern completion, quantitative concepts and basic math activities, spatial concept comprehension, and basic vocabulary comprehension. The COGAT® consists of three sections (each called a "Battery": the Verbal Battery, Quantitative Battery, and Non-Verbal Battery) and contains 9 question types:

Verbal Battery: Picture Analogies, Picture Classification, Sentence Completion
Quantitative Battery: Number Series, Number Puzzles, Number Analogies
Non-Verbal Battery: Figure Matrices, Figure Classification, Paper Folding

The COGAT® Practice Question Set (p. 62) is organized by question type. We suggest referencing the nine question type labels listed on pages 95-98 in the Answer Key in order to gain a better understanding of the material in each question type. After your child completes the Practice Question Set, you can use the Answer Key to evaluate your child's strengths/weaknesses by question type.

You should also use pages 56-61 of the NNAT2®/ NNAT3® Practice Question Set and pages 80-89 of the OLSAT® Practice Question Set for additional practice for the COGAT®.

• OLSAT® (OTIS-LENNON SCHOOL ABILITY TEST®) LEVEL A

The OLSAT® Level A is given to children in Pre-K and Kindergarten and lasts approximately one hour. It has 60 questions. Children at the Kindergarten level complete 60 questions, while children at the Pre-K level complete 40 questions. Check with your school to determine which version will be administered.

The test is in black-and-white. (Color books like this one cost more to print. However, we have found color images more engaging for kids, thereby facilitating learning. As a result, we include color images in this book. However, to give your child experience with the OLSAT® format, we have included some black-and-white questions in the OLSAT® Practice Question Set.)

The OLSAT® measures a child's ability to: classify objects, identify similarities/differences, figure out analogies, remember numbers/words, follow directions, determine sequences, complete patterns, and solve basic math problems. The verbal section also tests basic vocabulary as well as use of prepositions, spatial concepts, comparative terms, and ranking terms.

The OLSAT® has 10 question types:
Following Directions, Aural Reasoning, Arithmetic Reasoning, Picture Classification, Figure Classification, Picture Analogies, Figure Analogies, Pattern Matrix, Picture Series, and Figure Series.

The OLSAT® Practice Question Set (p. 80) is organized by question type. We suggest referencing the 10 question type labels listed on pages 98-101 in the Answer Key to gain a better understanding of the material in each question type. After your child has completed the Practice Question Set, you can use the Answer Key to evaluate your child's strengths/weaknesses by question type.

You should also use pages 56-61 of the NNAT2®/ NNAT3® Practice Question Set and pages 62-65, 68-75, 78-79 of the COGAT® Practice Question Set for additional practice for the OLSAT®.

TEST-TAKING TIPS

Listening Skills: Have your child practice listening carefully to questions and following the directions in this book. Paying attention is important, because often test questions are not repeated by the test administrator.

Negative Words: If your child will take a test with verbal sections (like the COGAT® or OLSAT®), (s)he should listen carefully for "negative words" ("no", "not", "nor", "neither") and negative prefixes like "un-".

Work Through The Exercise: In the Workbook section of this book, go through the exercises together by talking about them: what the exercise is asking the child to do and what makes the answer choices correct/incorrect. This will not only familiarize your child with working through exercises, it will also help him/her develop a process of elimination (getting rid of any answer choices that are incorrect).

Answer Choices: Make sure your child looks at **each** answer choice. You may wish to point to each answer choice if you notice your child not looking at each one.

Guessing: For the tests outlined in this book, test-takers receive points for the number of correct answers. It is advantageous to at least guess instead of leaving a question unanswered. If your child says that (s)he does not know the answer, (s)he should first eliminate any answers that are obviously not correct. Then, (s)he can guess from those remaining.

Choose ONE Answer: Remind your child to choose only ONE answer. If your child has a test with "answer bubbles," remind him/her that he/she must fill in only ONE bubble per question. If your child must instead point to an answer, remind him/her to point to only one answer per question.

Common Sense Tips: Children are like adults when it comes to common sense exam-readiness for test day. Make sure your child:

- is familiar with the test site (If the exam will be at a location that is new to your child, go to the testing site together before test day. Simply driving by or walking by the outside of the building not only ensures you know how to reach the site; it also will give your child a sense of familiarity, come test day.)
- is well-rested
- has eaten a breakfast for sustained energy and concentration (complex carbohydrates and protein; avoid foods/drinks high in sugar)
- has a chance to use the restroom prior to the test (The administrator may not allow a break during the test.)

Try not to get overly-stressed about the gifted testing process (as difficult as that may be). It is surprising how much children can sense from adults, and children learn best through play. So, the more fun that you can make test prep (by using something like a detective theme!), the better.

THE GIFTED DETECTIVE AGENCY *(Read this page with your child.)*

Alex

May

Sophie

Anya

Freddie

Max

We're the Gifted Detective Agency. We need another member, someone else to join us. We think YOU have what it takes!

"What does a detective do?" you may ask. Well, a detective figures out puzzles, solves problems, and finds answers to questions.

To prove you're ready to join the Gifted Detective Agency, you'll put your skills to the test in this book. Together with your mom, dad, or other adult, you need to solve puzzles. The adult helping you will explain what to do, so listen carefully!

A good detective:
- Pays attention and listens closely
- Looks carefully at all choices before answering a question
- Keeps trying even if some questions are hard

After you finish the questions on each page, mark the box at the bottom. Like this:

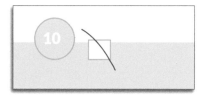 

Your parent (or other adult) will tell you which pages to do. After finishing them all, you will become a member of the Gifted Detective Agency! (Remember, it's more important to answer the questions the right way than to try to finish them really fast.) After you're done, you'll get your very own Gifted Detective Agency certificate.

When you're ready to start the puzzles, write your name here: _____

WILL YOU HELP ALEX ANSWER THESE QUESTIONS?

Directions: Look at the picture in the first box. Then, look at the group of pictures in the next box. Which picture from the group would go the best with the picture that is in the first box?

1.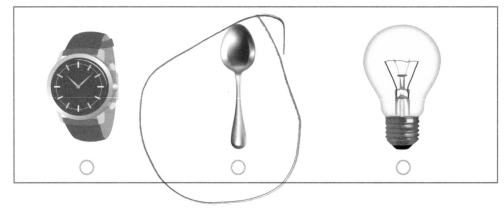

2.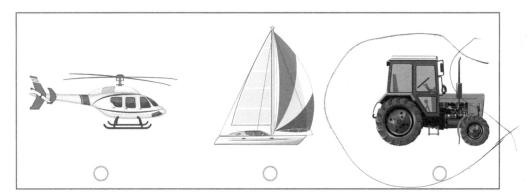

3.

LET'S HELP ALEX ANSWER THE SAME KIND OF QUESTION, BUT NOW WE'LL USE SHAPES!

4.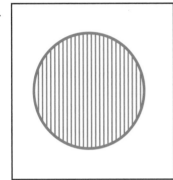

5.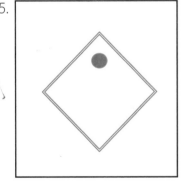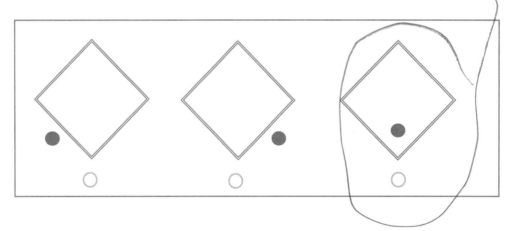

6.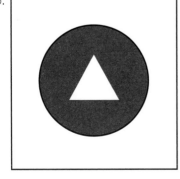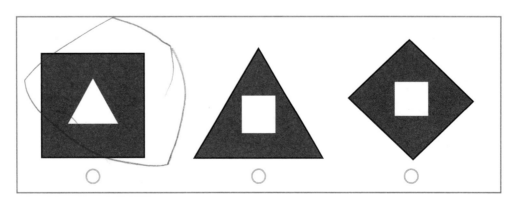

FREDDIE NEEDS YOUR HELP TO FIGURE OUT WHICH PICTURE DOESN'T BELONG!

Directions: Look at this row of pictures. One of these pictures in the row does not belong. This picture is not like the others in the row. Which picture does not belong?

7.

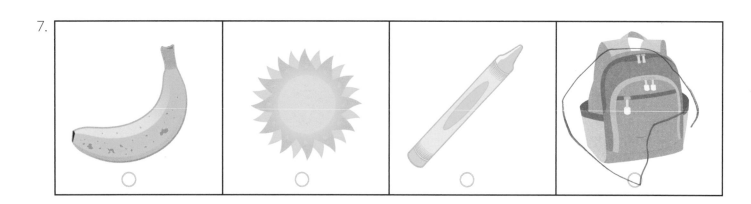

8.

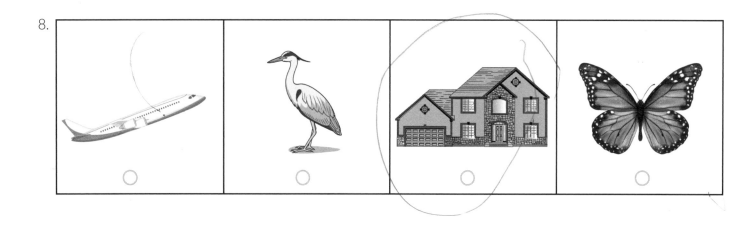

9.

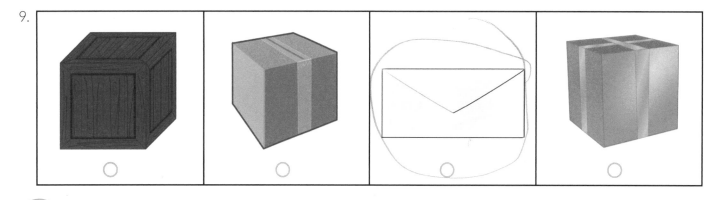

LET'S HELP FREDDIE ANSWER THE SAME KIND OF QUESTION, BUT NOW WE'LL USE SHAPES!

10.

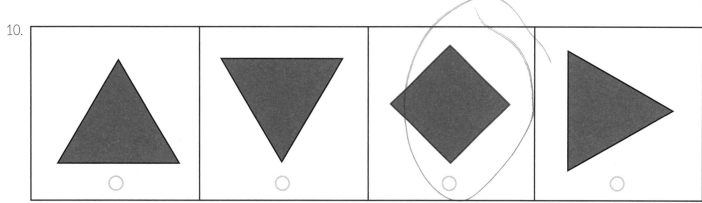

11.

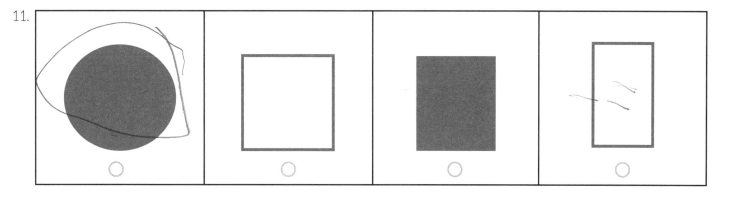

12.

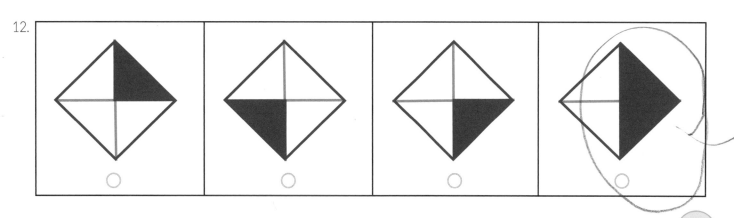

13

IT'S TIME TO HELP ANYA WITH MATCHING!

Directions: Look carefully at the top row of pictures. Each of these pictures is different in some way. (Point to the different pictures.) Draw a line from the picture on the top row to the picture on the bottom row that is exactly the same.

13.

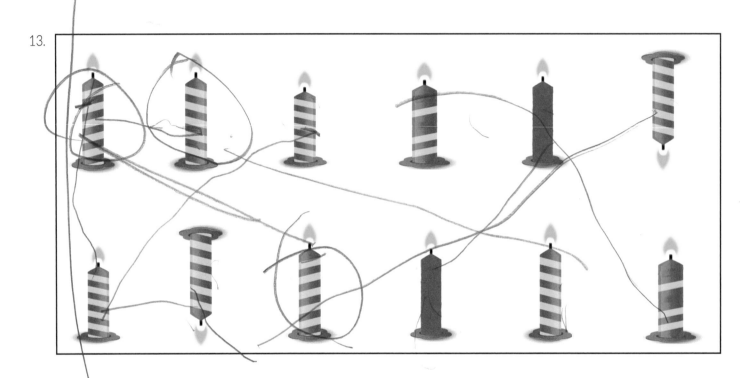

14.

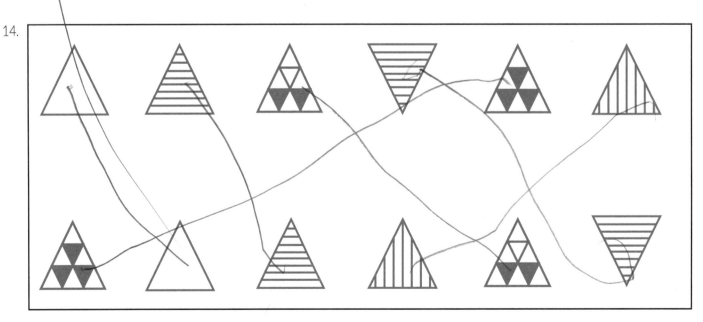

MAX NEEDS YOUR HELP WITH PATTERNS.

Directions: Look at this row of boxes. The pictures that are inside belong together in some way. Another picture should go inside the empty box. Under the boxes is a row of pictures. Which one should go in this empty box?

Example (read this to your child): Here is a row of boxes with queens and castles inside: queen - castle - queen - castle. What should go in the empty box to finish the pattern? (Go through answer choices together.) The queen should go in the empty box. That completes the pattern: queen-castle-queen-castle-queen.

15.

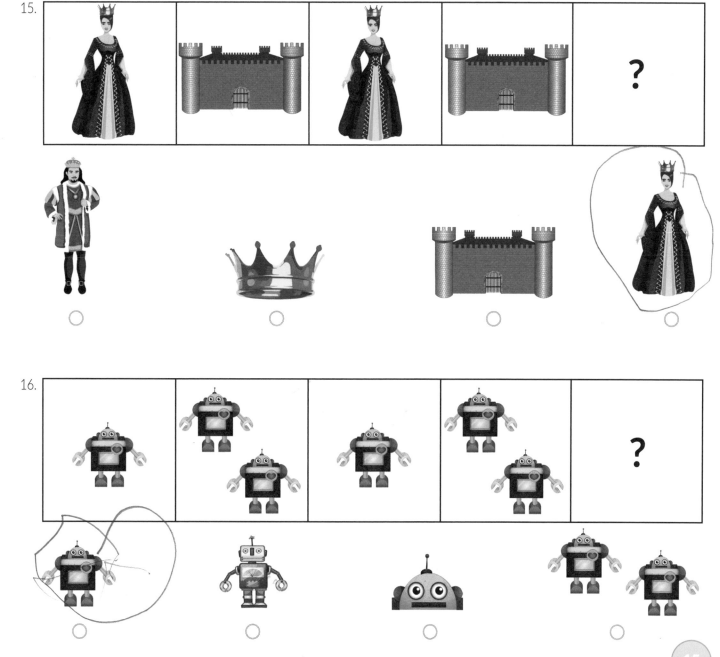

16.

17.

18.

19.

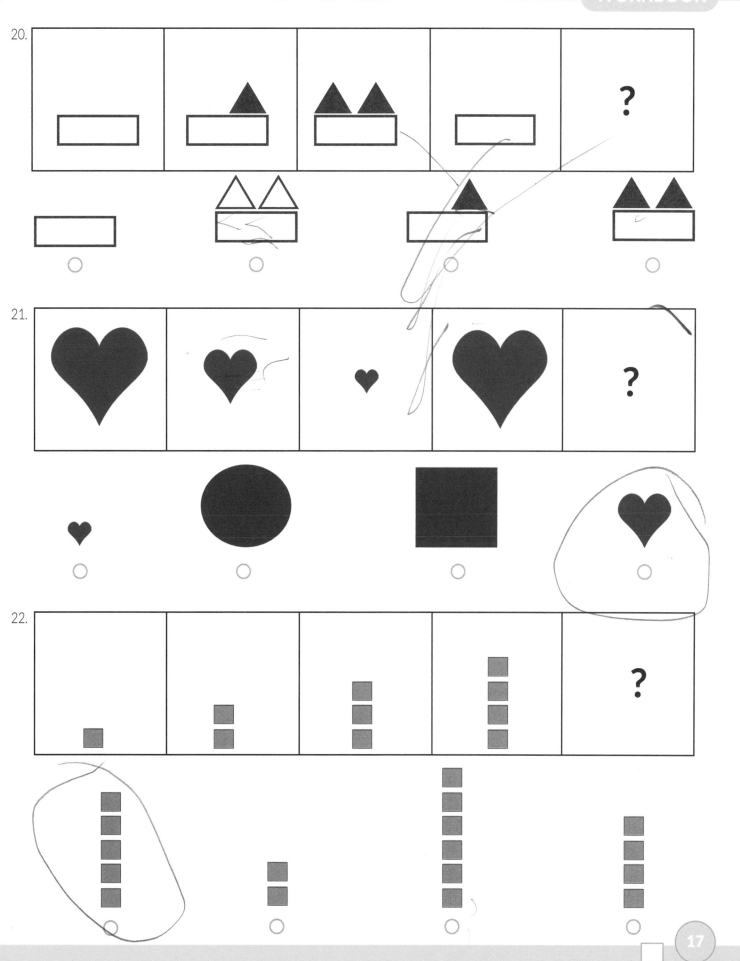

20.

21.

22.

HELP MAY FIGURE OUT WHAT GOES IN THE EMPTY BOX!

Directions: Look at these boxes that are on top. The pictures that are inside belong together in some way.

Then, look at these boxes that are on the bottom. One of these boxes on the bottom is empty.

Look next to the boxes. There is a row of pictures. Which one would go together with this picture that is in the bottom box like these pictures that are in the top boxes?

Parent note: Analogies are a new kind of "puzzle" for most young kids. They compare sets of items, and the way they are related can easily be missed at first. Work through these together with your child so (s)he sees how the top set is related. Together, try to come up with a "rule" to describe how the top set is related. Then, look at the picture on the bottom. Take this "rule," use it together with the picture on the bottom, and figure out which of the answer choices would follow that same rule.

Example (read this to your child): "Foot" is to "sock" as "hand" is to ___. (Talk about the two pictures on top and try to come up with a "rule.") The item in the first box goes inside the item in the second box. The item in the second box covers the item in the first box.

What about a hand? Which of the answer choices would do the same thing to a hand? What would a hand go inside? Which one would cover a hand?

(Go through answer choices and eliminate the incorrect ones first.) A glove! A hand goes inside a glove. A glove covers a hand.

23.

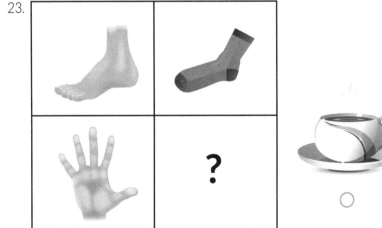   

24.

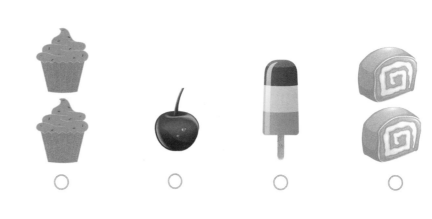

25.

26.

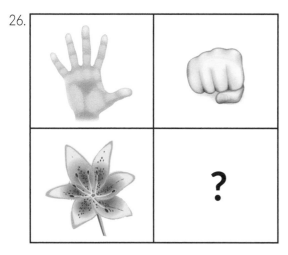

27.

28.

29.

30.

31.

LET'S HELP MAY ANSWER THE SAME KIND OF QUESTION ON THE NEXT PAGE, BUT NOW WE'LL USE SHAPES!

32.

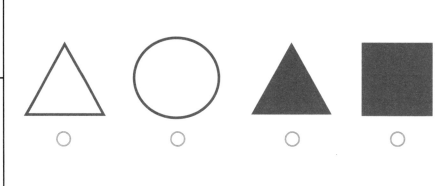

33.

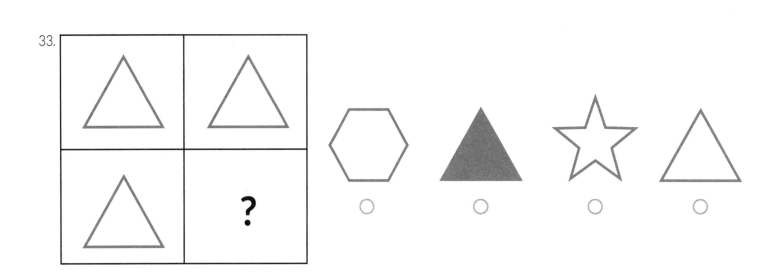

34.

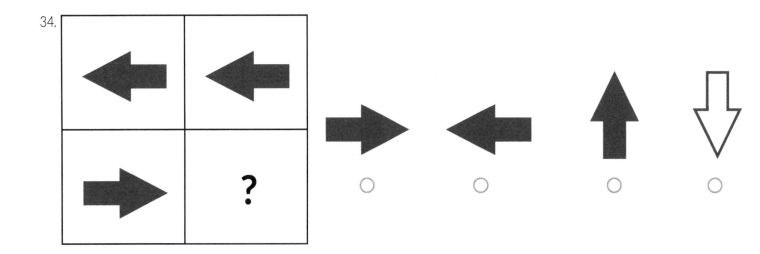

35.

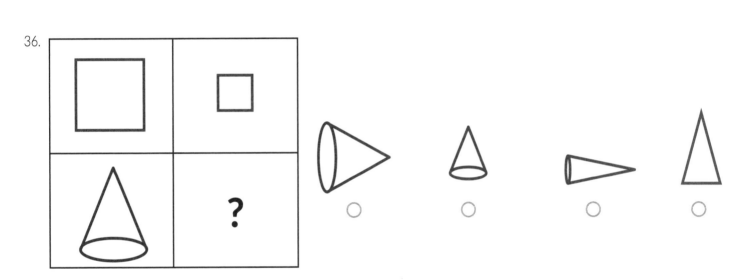

36.

37.

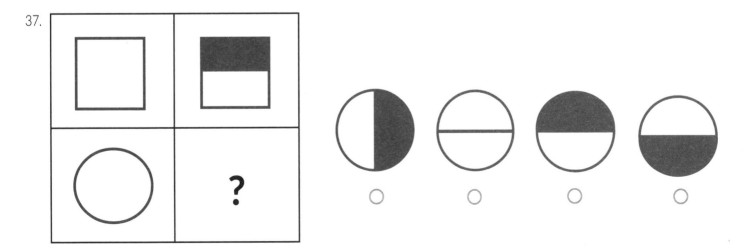

38.

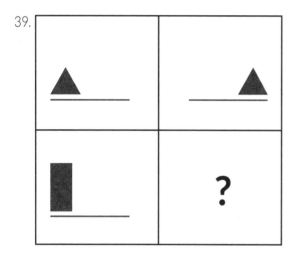

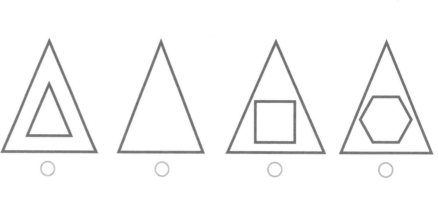

39.

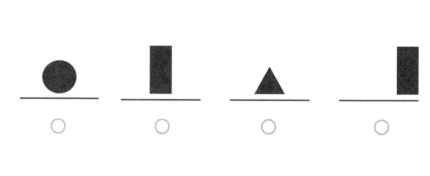

40.

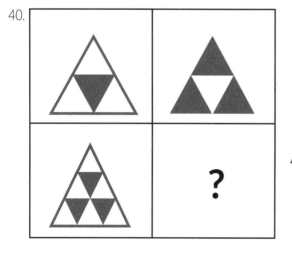

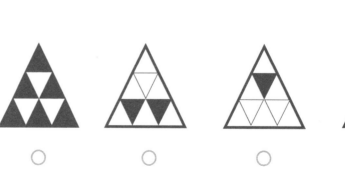

41.

○   ○   ○   ○

42.

○   ●   ●   ○

○   ○   ○   ●

○   ○   ●   ○

○   ○   ○   ○

NICE

WORK!

Directions: Look closely at these pictures that are inside the boxes. They make a pattern. Look at the last box. It is empty. Look next to the boxes. A row of pictures is next to the boxes. Which one should go inside the empty box in the bottom row?

Example (read this to your child): Look at these pictures that are in the boxes across the different rows. They make a pattern. In the top row, there are 2 purple squares, 3 purple squares, and 2 purple squares. The shapes are the same and form a pattern: 2-3-2. There is the same pattern in the next row with the purple hexagons: 2-3-2. In the bottom row, there are 2 purple diamonds, 3 purple diamonds, and ___. What would go in the last box? (Go through choices.) Two purple diamonds go in the last box. They complete the pattern: 2-3-2.

(Parent note: The columns also have a pattern which your child may pick up on. In the first column there are 2 shapes of each: 2 purple squares, 2 purple hexagons, and 2 diamonds. In the second column there is also a pattern of 3 shapes each: 3 purple squares, 3 purple hexagons, 3 purple diamonds. In the last column, there is also a pattern of 2 shapes each: 2 purple squares, 2 purple hexagons, and 2 purple diamonds.)

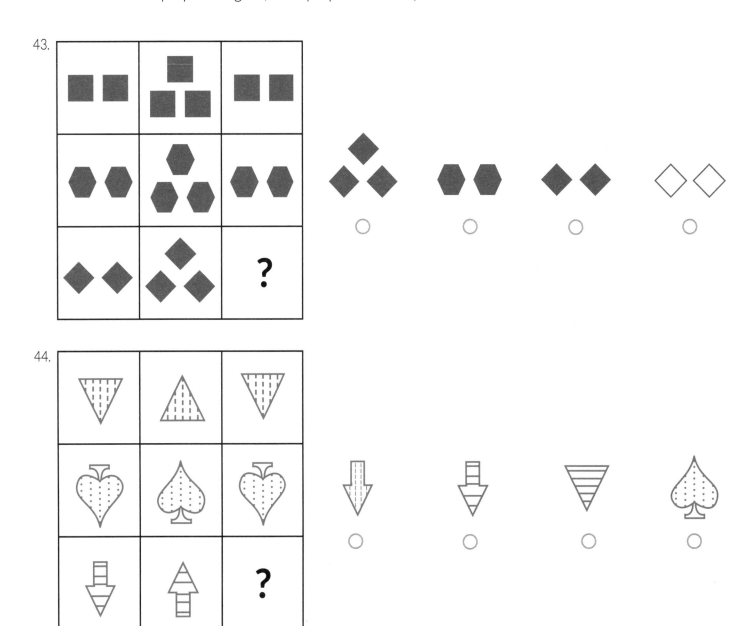

45.

○ ○ ○ ○

46.

○ ○ ○ ○

47.

○ ○ ○ ○

FREDDIE SAYS, "YOU'RE DOING GREAT. LET'S DO SOME MORE PUZZLES!"

Directions: Look at these pictures that are inside the boxes. These belong together in some way. One box is missing. (Point to the bottom box that has a question mark.)

Now, look below at the row of answer choices. (Point to the row of answer choices.)

Which one would go here? (Point to the bottom box that has a question mark again.)

48.

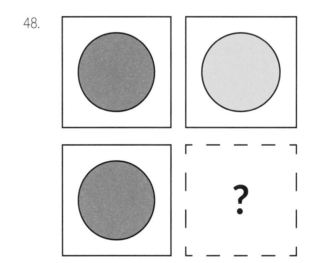

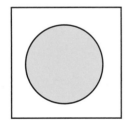
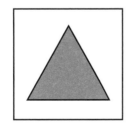

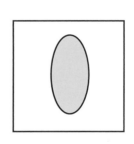
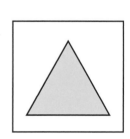

49.

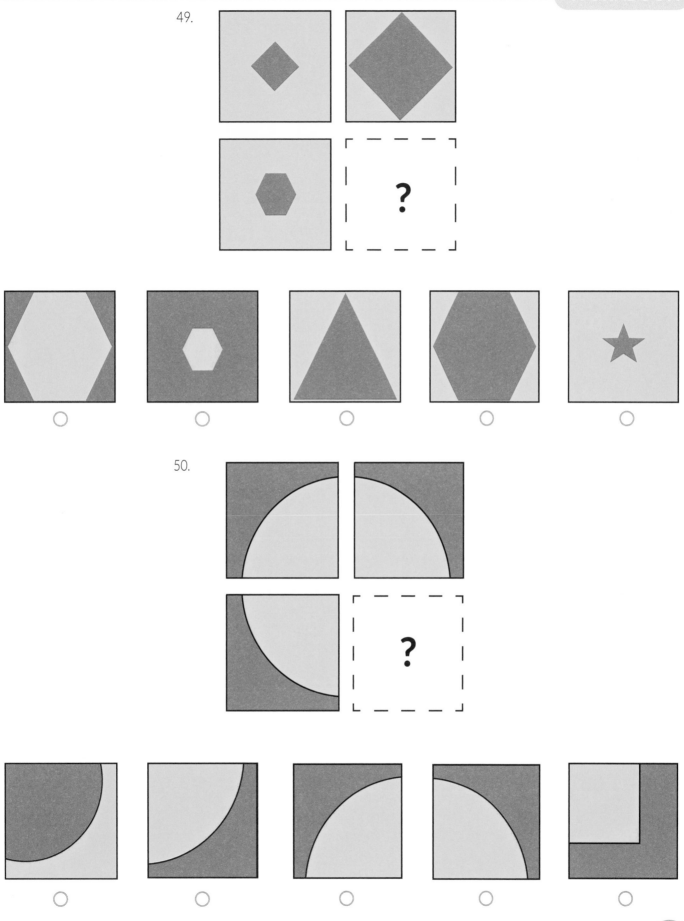

50.

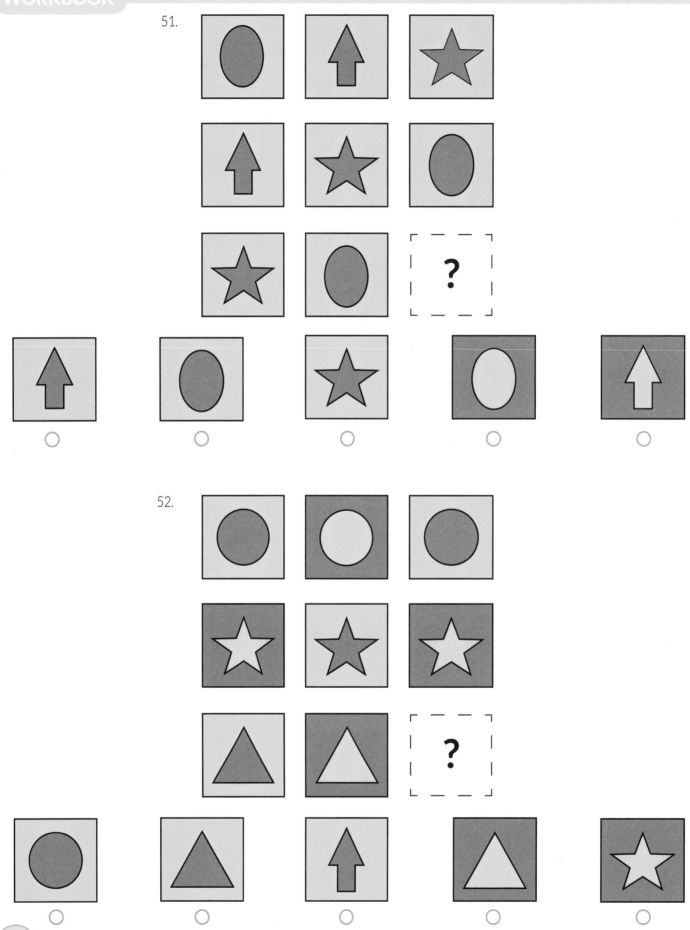

51.

52.

ALEX NEEDS YOUR HELP TO FIND THINGS. LISTEN UP!

Section explanation: These exercises will test your child's ability to use prepositions, comparative terms, ranking terms, quantitative terms, "negative" words, basic vocabulary, as well as his/her memory, listening skills, and reasoning skills. Try to read each item only <u>once</u> to your child.

Directions for 53-55 (ocean scene) : I am going to ask you to find some animals in the picture below. I can only read these one time, so listen carefully. (Do each letter one at a time.)

53.

A) Red fish next to a yellow fish

B) Three identical fish together

54.

C) A fish with spots above a fish with stripes

D) Spotted fish below a striped fish

55.

E) A group of fish where two purple fish are on top and one orange fish is on the bottom

F) A dolphin that's upside down

Directions for the rest: Listen to the question and then choose your answer.

56. Which one shows two shells of the same size and two frogs of different sizes?

57. Which one shows a pirate first, a starfish second, and a boat last?

58. Which one shows three balls that are exactly the same and on the same side of the bucket?

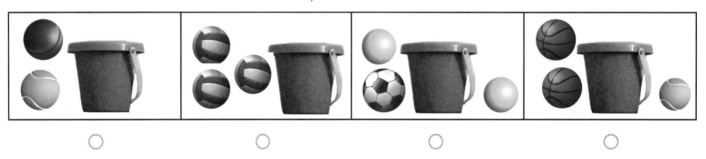

59. Which one shows two upside-down umbrellas with a ball in the middle?

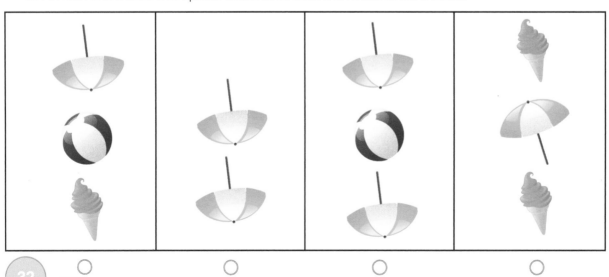

60. Which one would you find on a boat?

    ○   ○   ○   ○

61. Which one would sink in the water?

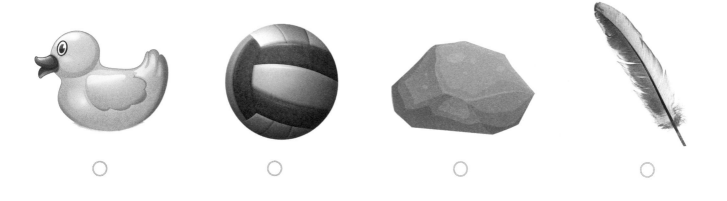

    ○   ○   ○   ○

62. Which choice shows one thing that walks on land and one thing that floats on water?

    ○   ○   ○   ○

63. Which one would someone <u>not</u> wear at the beach?

○ ○ ○ ○

64. Which animal would you <u>not</u> find in the water?

○ ○ ○ ○

65. Which one shows a pair?

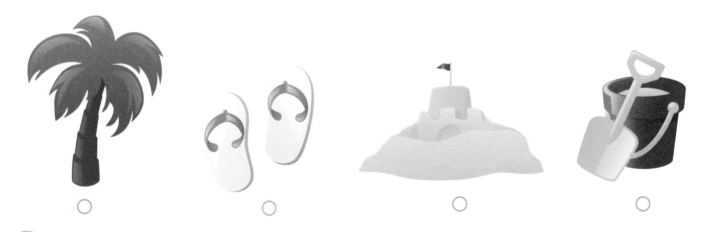

○ ○ ○ ○

66. Look at this picture on the left. Which answer choice shows the animal that is inside both the square and the circle?

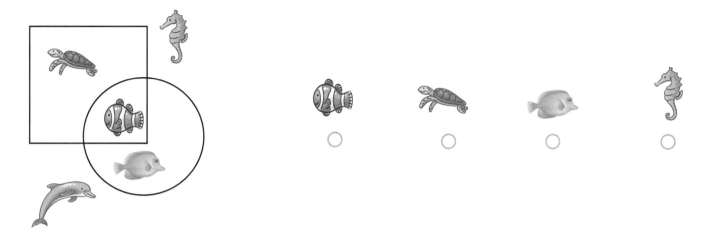

67. Look at this picture on the left. Which answer choice shows the animal that is in neither the triangle nor the circle?

68. Look at this picture on the left. Which answer choice shows the animal that is inside the triangle but not inside the circle?

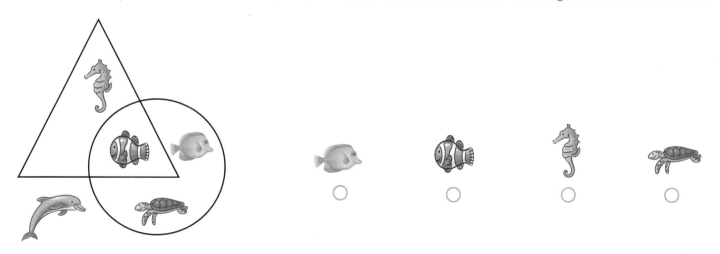

LET'S GIVE ANYA A HIGH FIVE AND HELP HER WITH THESE QUESTIONS.

Section explanation: An abacus is a toy with rods and beads that is used for counting. Here, the final rod of the abacus is missing. The first five rods of the abacus have a pattern. Have your child look closely at these five to determine the pattern. The last rod (the sixth rod) is missing. (S)he will then need to select which rod would finish the pattern. Make sure your child carefully and correctly counts the number of abacus beads. Note that some answer choices do not have any beads. This equals "0". Due to the complexity of this question type, we have included detailed directions for the first question.

Directions for first question: Here's an abacus. The "circles" on the abacus are beads. These beads are on rods. The beads in the first five rods have made a pattern. Look at the last rod on the abacus. The beads on this rod are missing.

Next to the abacus are three rods. These are the answer choices. Choose which rod would go in the place of the last rod in order to complete the pattern.

Let's look at the abacus. Do you see a pattern? It is: 2 beads - 1 bead - 2 beads - 1 bead - 2 beads, and __. What comes next? (Look at each answer choice.) It is 1 bead. This completes the pattern: 2-1-2-1-2-1.

Directions for the rest: Which rod would go in the place of the missing rod to finish the pattern?

69.

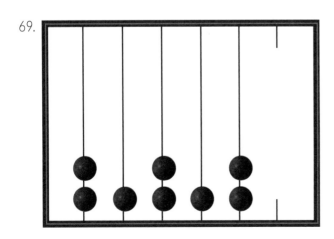

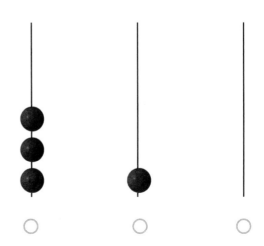

70.

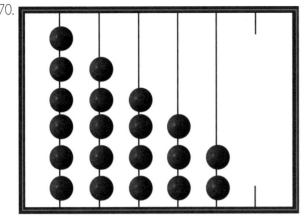

71.

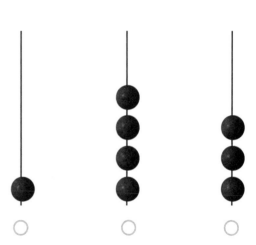

72.

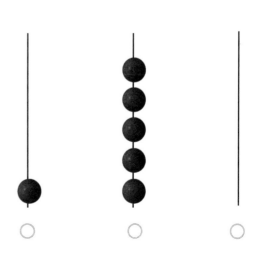

MAX NEEDS YOUR HELP WITH THESE NUMBER GAMES!

Section explanation: Here are two trains: one on the top and one on the bottom. Each train must have the same total number of items. (In this workbook section they are presents.) Your child needs to figure out which train car among the answer choices would go in place of the car(s) with the question mark. The train on the top must have the same total number of items as the one on the bottom. Make sure your child carefully and correctly counts the number of items. Due to the complexity of this question type, we have included detailed directions for the first question.

Directions for first question: Look at the first train, the one on the top. It has 2 presents.

Look at the train on the bottom, the second train. This train has 1 present. You need to put a train car in place of the train car that has a question mark so that the second train has the same number as the other train.

Which train car should you choose so that the second train has 2 presents all together? It would be the train car that has 1 present. One plus one equals two. Now the two trains would have the same number.

Directions for the rest: Which train car should you choose so that the second train has the same number of presents as the first?

73.

○ ○ ○

74.

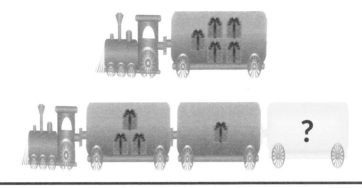

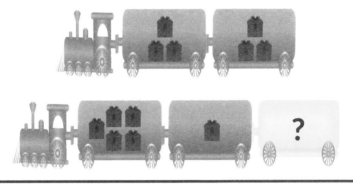

　　　○　　　　　　　　○　　　　　　　　○

75.

　　　○　　　　　　　　○　　　　　　　　○

76.

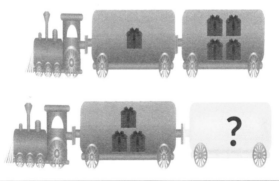

　　　○　　　　　　　　○　　　　　　　　○

FREDDIE NEEDS A HAND WITH NUMBER GAMES!

Section explanation: Number analogies questions are similar to the other analogy questions earlier in this book. Here, however, the top set of boxes and the bottom set of boxes must have the same type of quantitative relationship. Your child must figure out which one of the answer choices would go in the empty box with the question mark to complete the mathematical analogy. Due to the complexity of this section, we have included detailed directions for the first question.

Directions for first question: Let's look carefully at these pictures in the top row. These pictures belong together in some way. There are four acorns in the left box. There are two acorns in the right box. What has changed between the picture on the left and the picture on the right? We need to come up with a "rule" to describe what has happened. This box has two fewer acorns than the first box. Two acorns were taken away from the first box to get the number of acorns in the second box.

Next, let's look carefully at the boxes in the bottom row. The first box has three squirrels. The second box is empty. Look carefully at the row of pictures next to the boxes. Which one of these goes in the empty box? The answer is "one squirrel." On the bottom row, the first box has three squirrels. If you take away two (the way you took away two in the top row), then you have one squirrel.

Directions for the rest: Which answer choice would go inside the empty box at the bottom?

77.

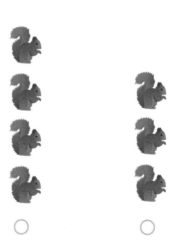

○   ○   ○

78.

○   ○   ○

79.

80.

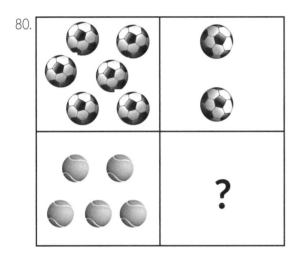

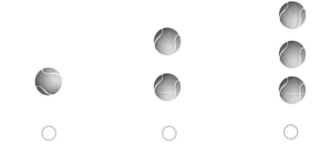

81.

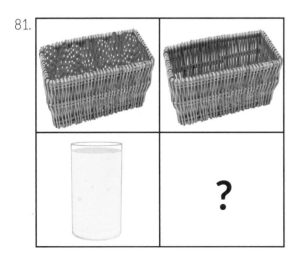

LET'S HELP ANYA AND ALEX AT THE TOY STORE!

Directions: Listen to the question and then choose your answer. (Parents, try to read each question only one time so your child can practice listening skills. Each question is above the corresponding set of boxes.)

82. Alex has the number of robots in the first box. Anya has one more robot than Alex has. Which box shows how many robots Anya has?

83. Anya wants to buy five teddy bears, but she has only found the number of teddy bears in the first box. How many more teddy bears does Anya need to find so that she will have five?

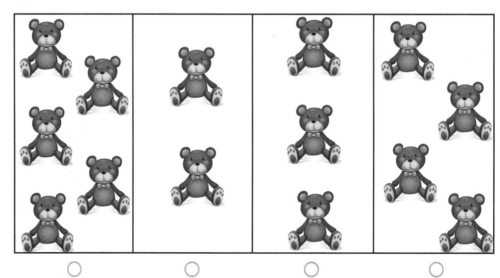

84. The toy store has the number of balloons in the first box. Then, Alex pops half of the balloons. Which box shows how many of the balloons Alex popped?

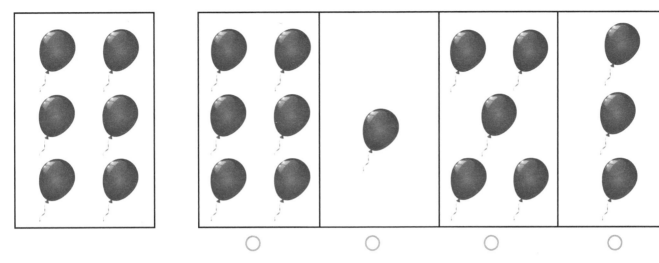

85. Anya buys the number of trains in the first box. Alex buys more trains than Anya buys. Which box shows how many trains Alex buys?

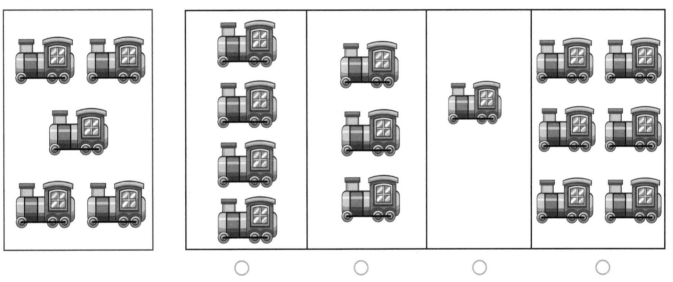

86. Anya buys the number of beach balls in the first box. Alex also buys beach balls, but he buys fewer of them than Anya buys. Which box shows how many beach balls Alex buys?

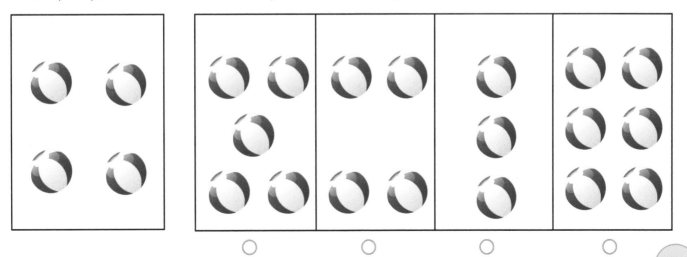

WILL YOU HELP MAY FINISH THESE PUZZLES?

Directions: Here is a puzzle where a piece is missing. (Point to the box that has the question mark.) Which one of the answer choices (point to the row of answer choices) would go here? (Point to the box that has the question mark again.)

Parent note: Help your child complete these by asking him/her to look closely at the colors and lines (and in some cases, shapes) of the puzzle. Then, (s)he should do the same with the area around the white box. How do the colors/lines/shapes look next to the white box?

Ask your child what (s)he thinks the puzzle would look like below the white box, if (s)he could pick it up.

87.

88.

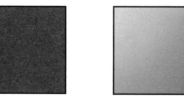

NOW LET'S TRY SOME WITH SHAPES AND LINES.

89.

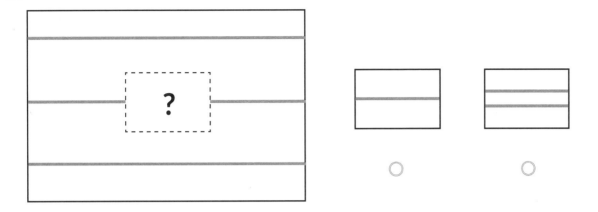

90.

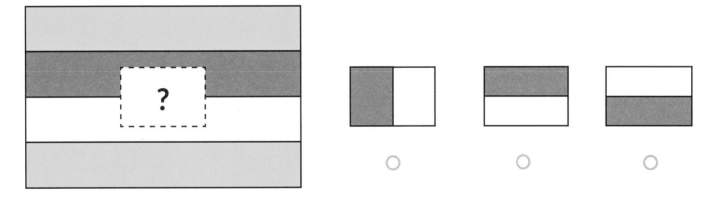

91.

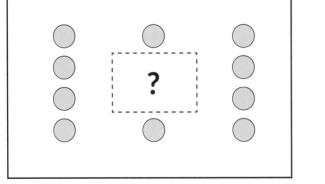 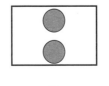 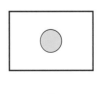 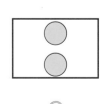

92.

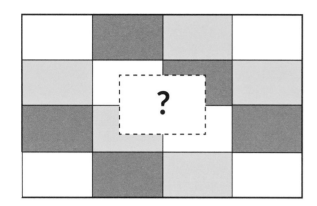

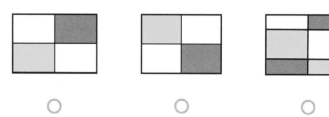

93.

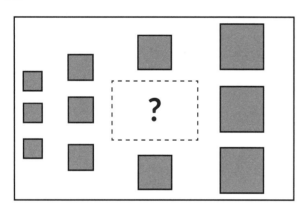

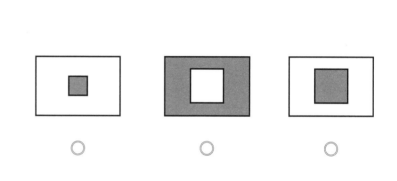

94.

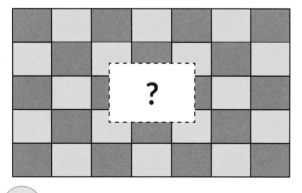

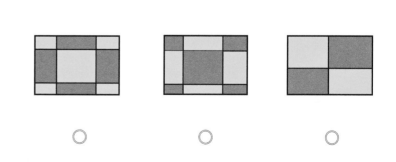

LET'S GIVE SOPHIE A HAND!

Directions: Look at the top row of pictures. These show a sheet of paper and how it was folded. Look at these pictures that are on the bottom row. Which picture shows how the paper would look after the paper is unfolded?

Parent note: The paper folding exercises may be difficult at first for your child. If so, go through the exercises together using a real sheet of paper.

95.

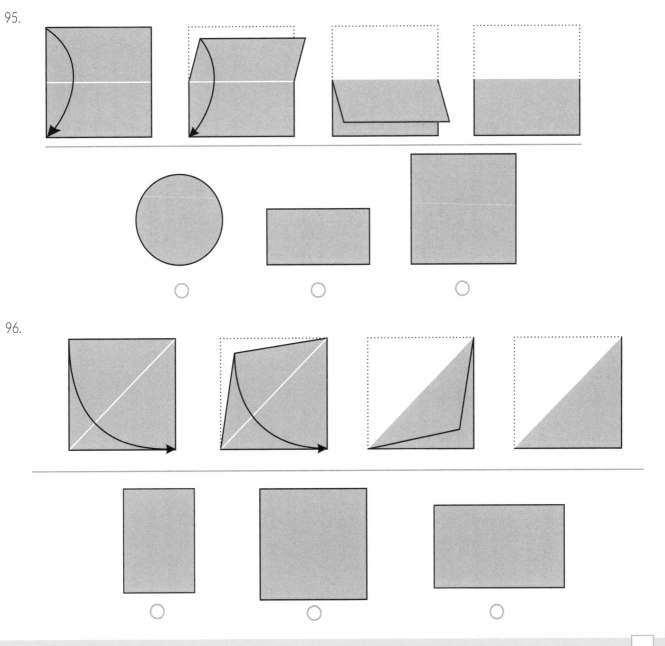

96.

YOU'RE GOING TO BE A GREAT DETECTIVE!

Directions: Look at the top row of pictures. These show a sheet of paper, how it was folded, and how holes were made in the folded sheet of paper. Look at these pictures that are on the bottom row. Which picture shows how the paper would look after the paper is unfolded?

Parent note: To help your child better understand these exercises, demonstrate using real paper and a hole puncher (or scissors). Be sure to point out the placement of the holes and the number of holes you make in the paper.

97.

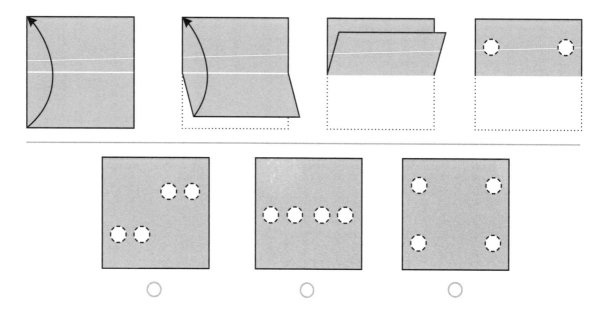

98.

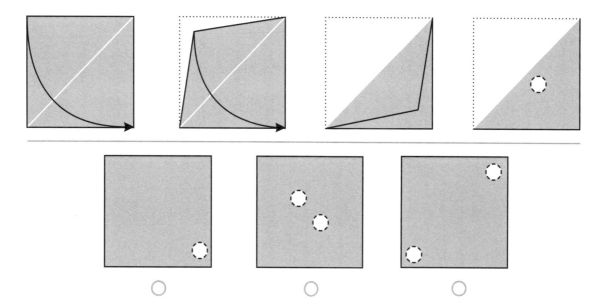

LET'S HELP SOPHIE WITH A FEW MORE!

Directions: Look at the top row of pictures. These show a sheet of paper and how it was folded. The picture with the scissors shows where a part of the folded sheet of paper was cut out. On the bottom row, which picture shows how the sheet of paper would look after the paper is unfolded?

Parent note: To help your child better understand these exercises, demonstrate using real paper and scissors. Be sure to point out the placement of the part that is cut out.

99.

100.

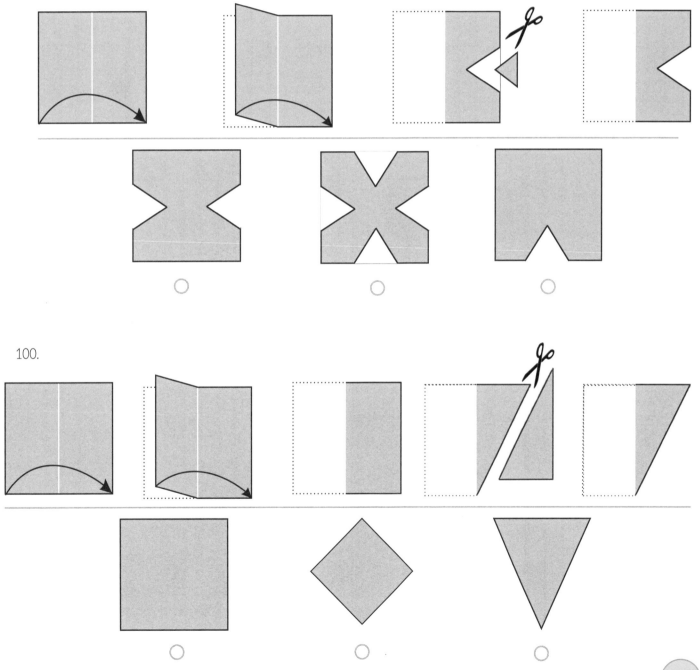

PRACTICE QUESTION SETS INSTRUCTIONS

✂ Please cut out pages 93-101. (These pages are: the Answer Key for the Workbook and the Directions & Answer Key for the Practice Question Sets.)

Reading Directions: Tell your child to listen carefully (like a detective!), because you can read the directions to him/her only one time. (Test administrators often read directions only once.)

Test instructors will not let your child know if his/her answers are correct/incorrect. If you wish for the Practice Question Sets to serve as a "practice test," then as your child completes the Practice Question Sets, we suggest you do the same. Instead of saying if answers are correct/incorrect, you could say something like, "Nice work, let's try some more."

Navigation Figures: Assuming your child has completed the Workbook, then (s)he is familiar with exercise format (navigating through pages with rows of questions). To make test navigation easier for kids, some gifted tests use image markers in place of question numbers and in place of page numbers.

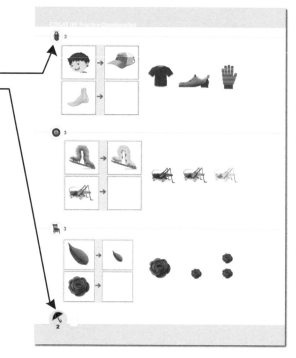

We include these "markers" in the OLSAT® and COGAT® Practice Question Sets so that your child can be familiar with them.

When your child needs to look at a new page, you would say, for example, "Find the page where there is an umbrella at the bottom." When your child needs to look at a question, you would say, for example, "Find the row where there is a bug."

These markers are listed on the Directions & Answer Key pages for the OLSAT® and COGAT® so that you can read them to your child. The NNAT2®/ NNAT3® Practice Question Set does not have these.

"Bubbles" and Answer Choices: If your child is at the Kindergarten level, (s)he may have to fill in "bubbles" (the circles) to indicate answer choice. The Practice Question Sets have answer bubbles. If your child is at the Pre-K level, (s)he will most likely have to point to the answer choice. (Answer choices are indicated with corresponding letters in the Answer Key.)

Time: Allow one minute per question, approximately.

Evaluation: Each Practice Question Set is labeled by question type. After your child is done, on your own (without your child) go through the Set by question type, writing the number answered correctly in the space provided on the answer key. While these practice questions are not meant to be used in place of an official assessment, these will provide a general overview of strengths/weaknesses, as they pertain to test question type. For questions your child didn't answer correctly, go over the question and answer choices again with him/her. Compare the answer choices, specifically what makes the correct answer choice the right choice. Since gifted programs typically accept only top performers, you may wish to do additional practice. **We offer additional practice books as well as FREE questions. Please see page 102 (the last page in the book) for details.**

See the first page of directions of each Practice Question Set for more instructions: NNAT2®/ NNAT3® p. 94 , COGAT® p. 95, OLSAT® p. 98.

1

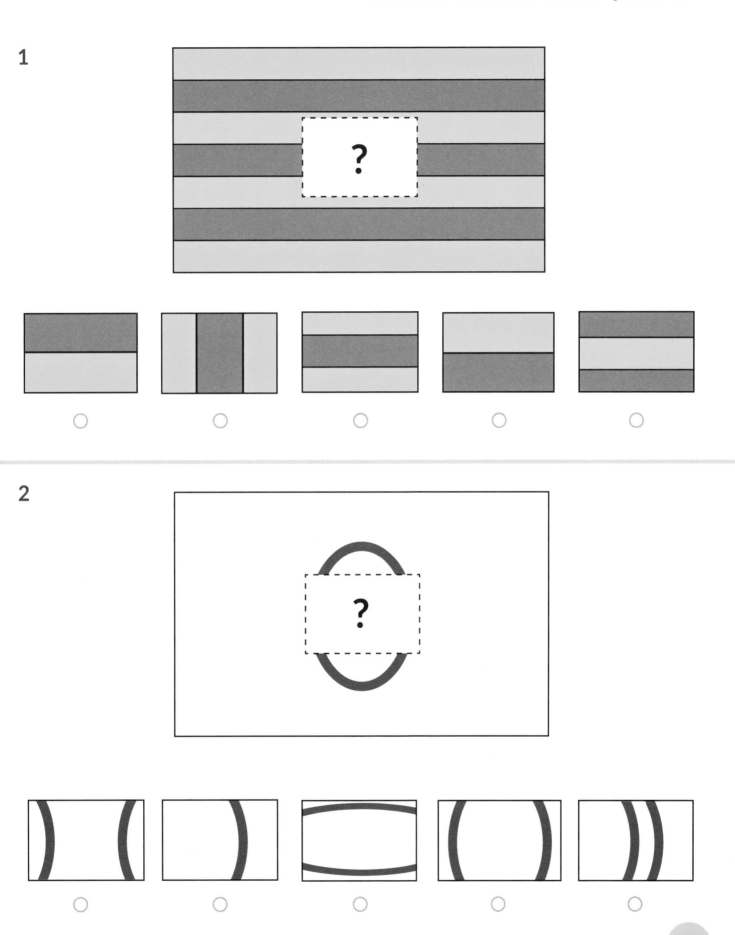

3

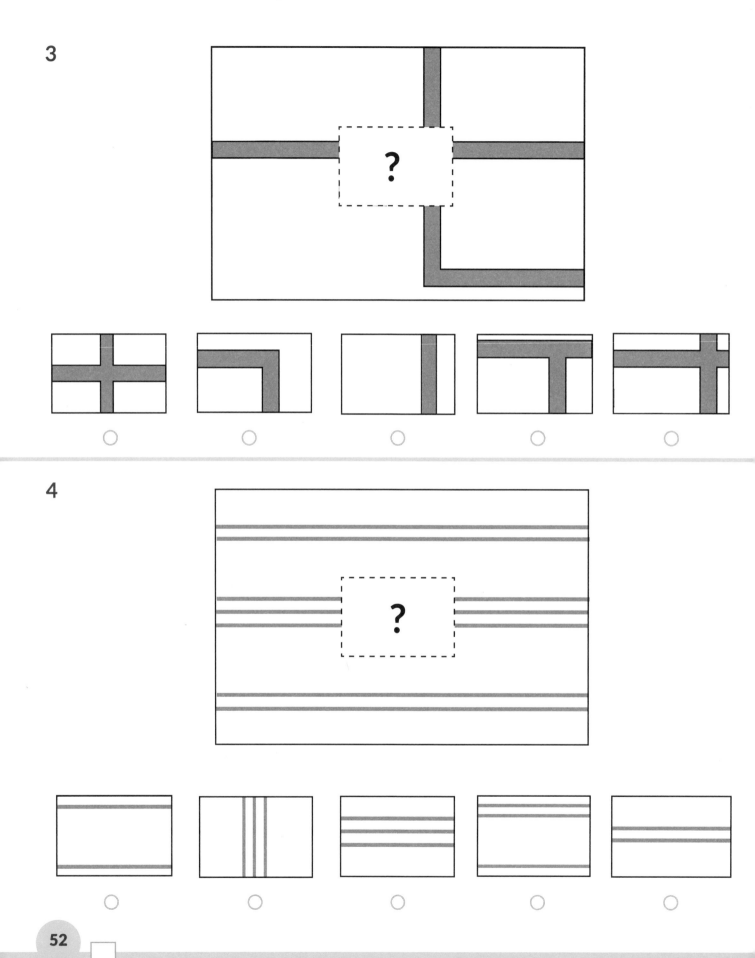

4

5

6

7

   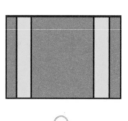 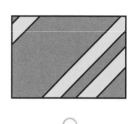

○   ○   ○   ○   ○

8

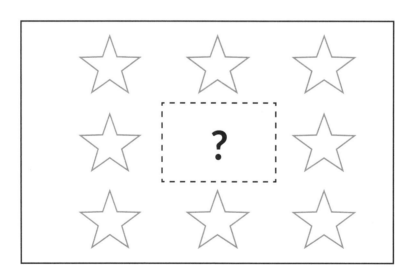

 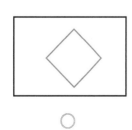   

○   ○   ○   ○   ○

9

10

11

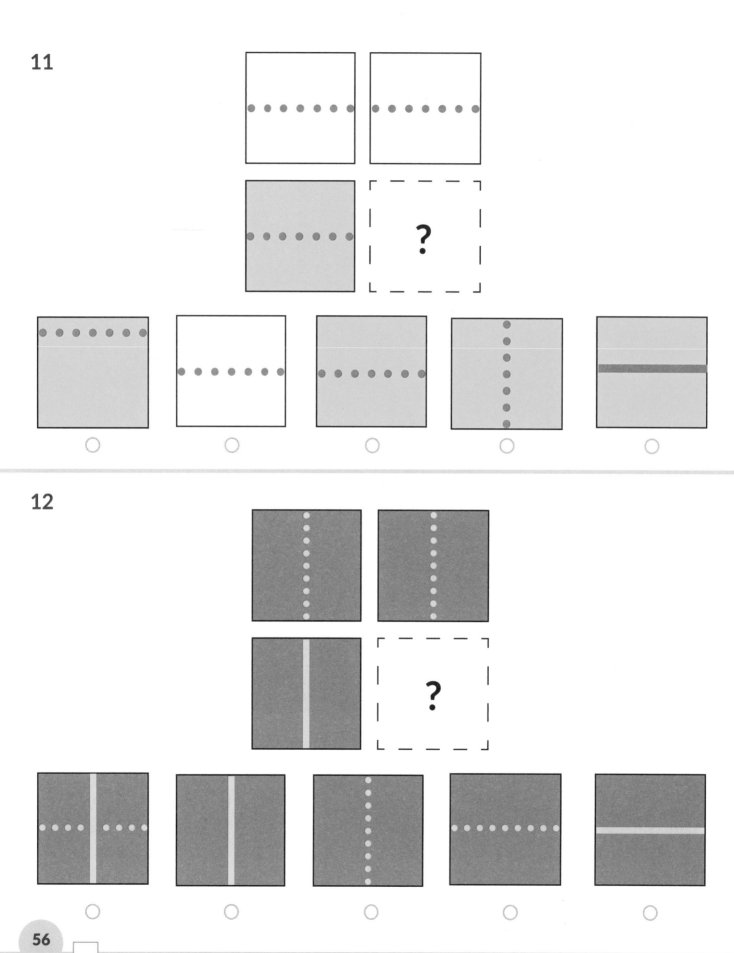

13

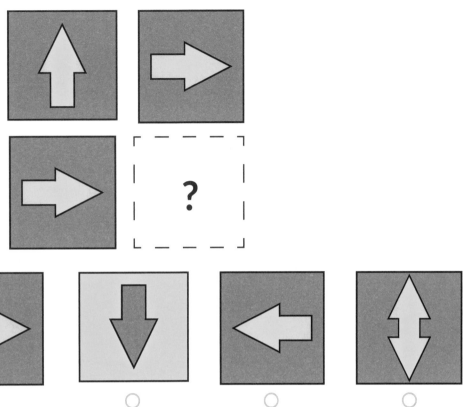

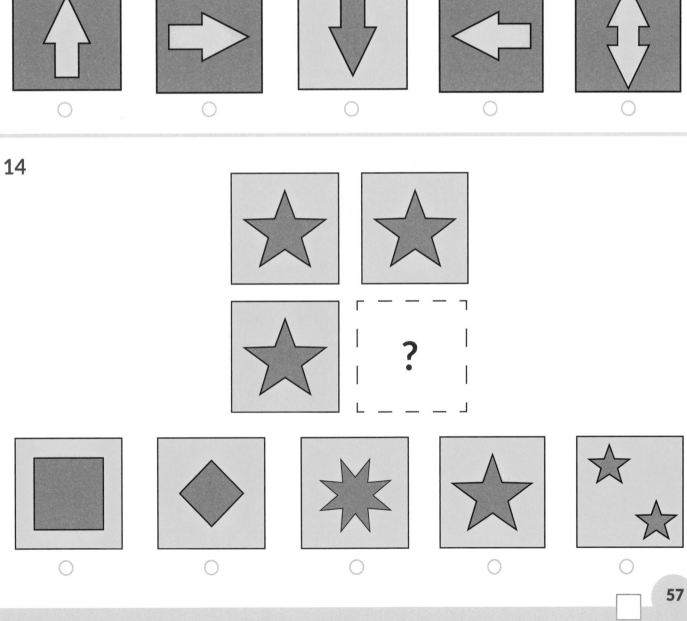

14

15

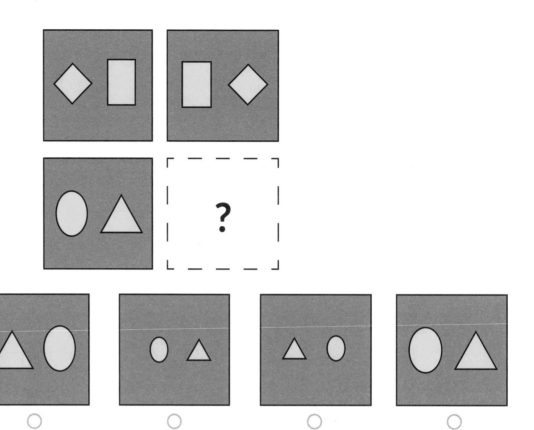

  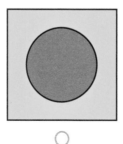 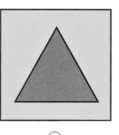 

○   ○   ○   ○   ○

16

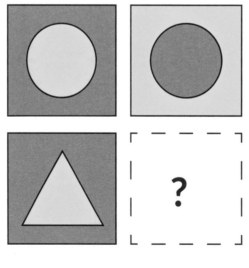

○   ○   ○   ○   ○

17

18

19

20

21

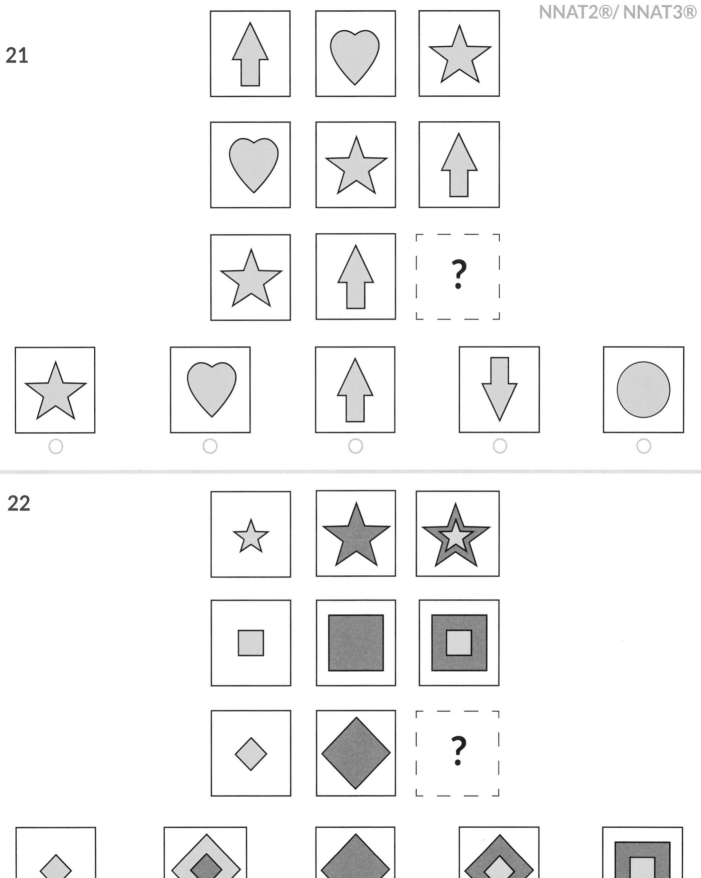

1

 ○

 ○

○

 2

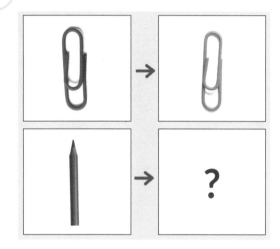

 ○

 ○

 ○

3

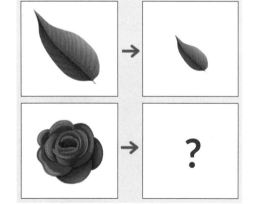

 ○

 ○

     ○

4

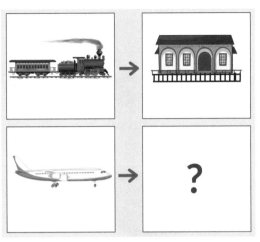

◯   ◯   ◯

 5

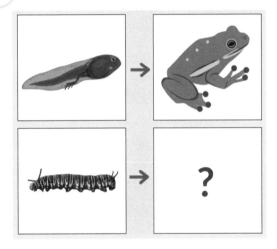

◯   ◯   ◯

 6

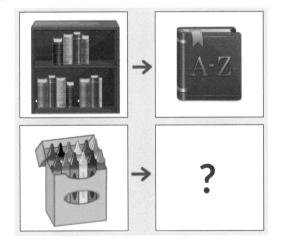

◯   ◯   ◯

7

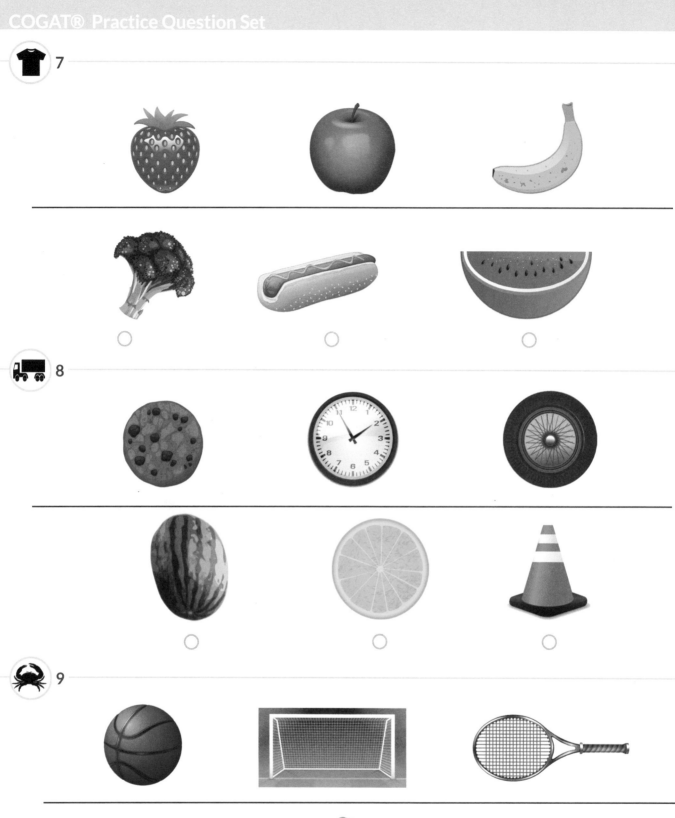

8

9

10

○ ○ ○

 11

○ ○ ○

 12

○ ○ ○

13

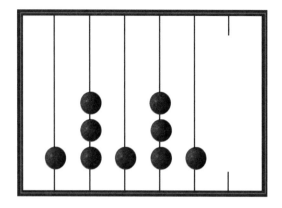 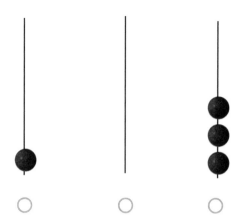

 14

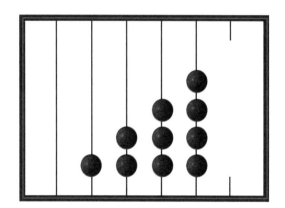 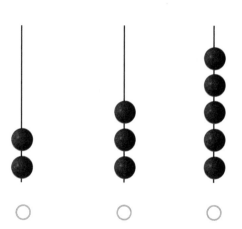

 15

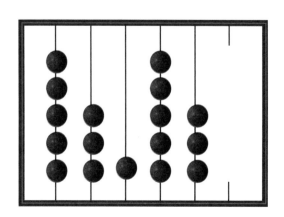 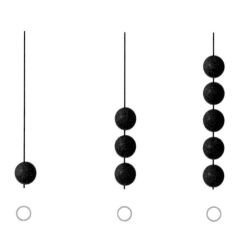

16

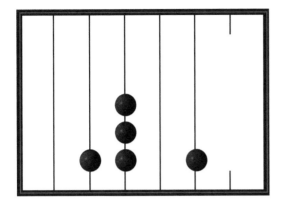

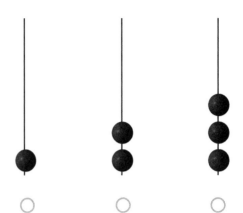

 17

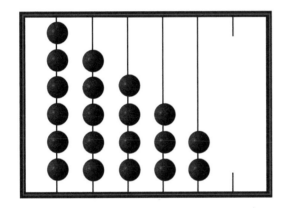

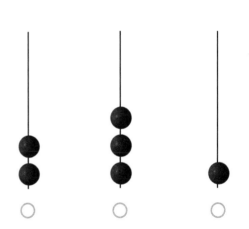

 18

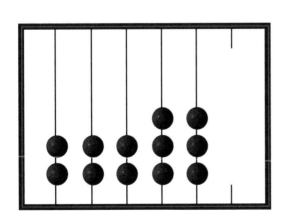

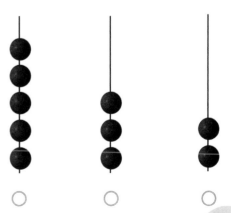

19

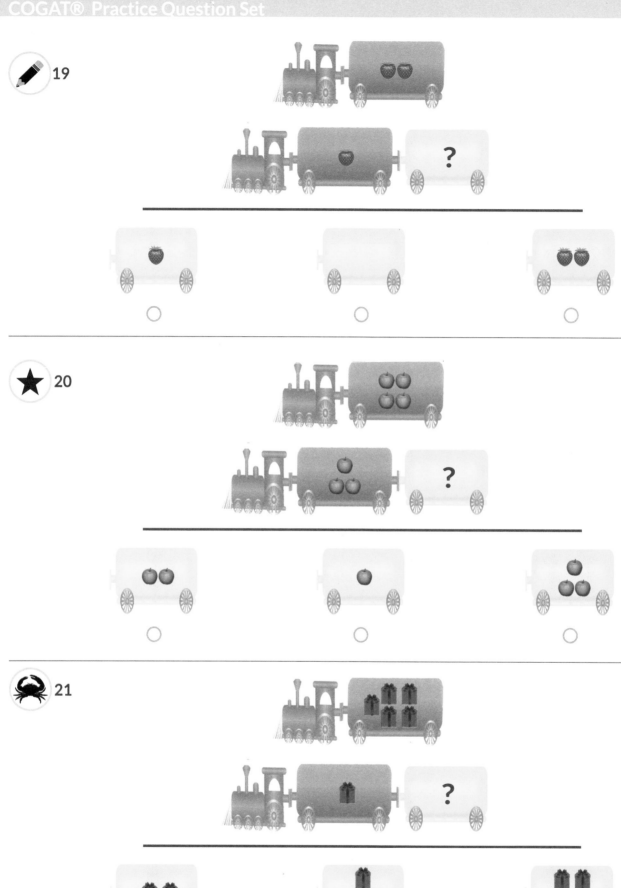

20

21

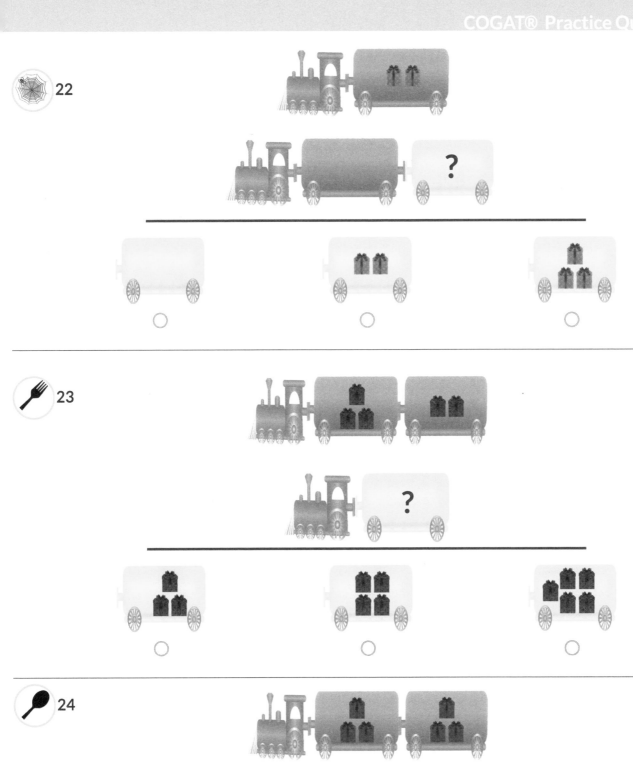

22

23

24

25

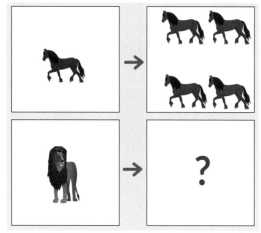

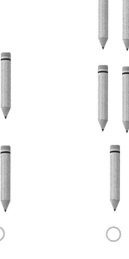

○   ○   ○

▲ 26

○   ○   ○

 27

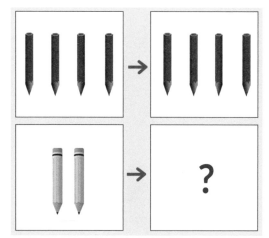

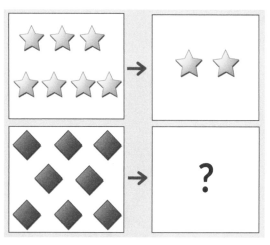

○   ○   ○

28

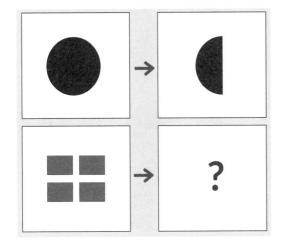

 29

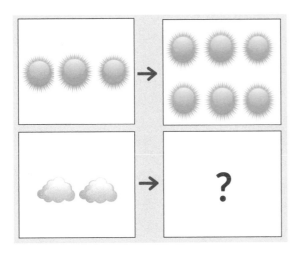

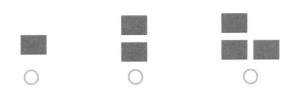

 30

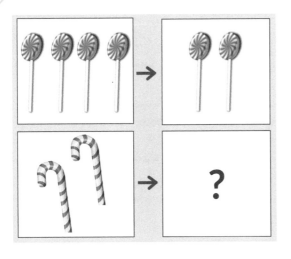

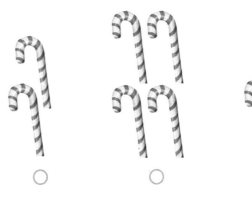

31

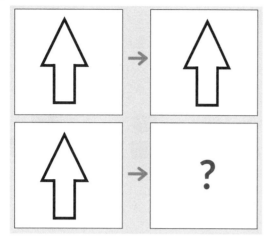

  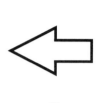

○   ○   ○

 32

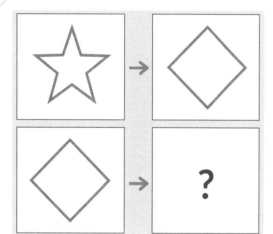

○   ○   ○

 33

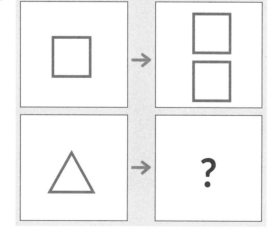

○   ○   ○

34

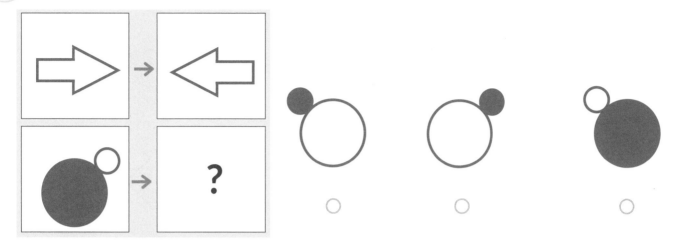

35

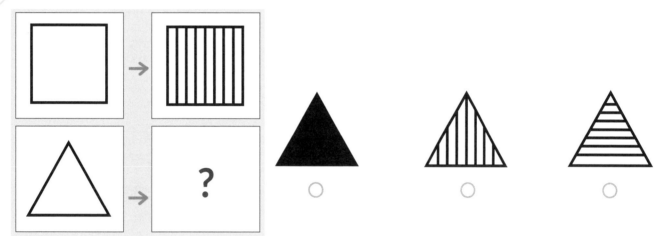

36

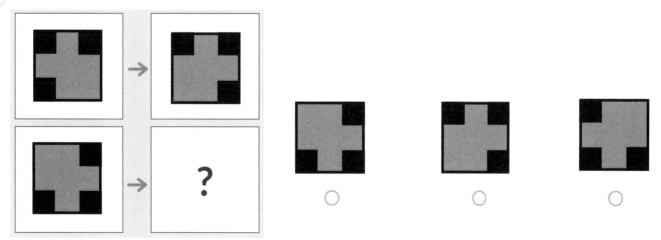

37

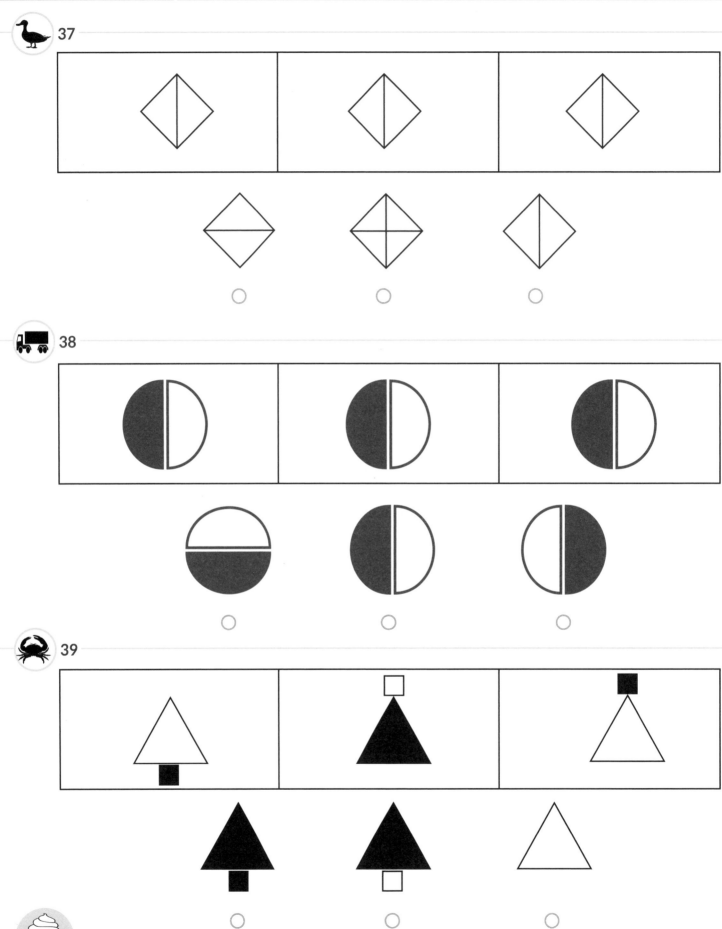

40

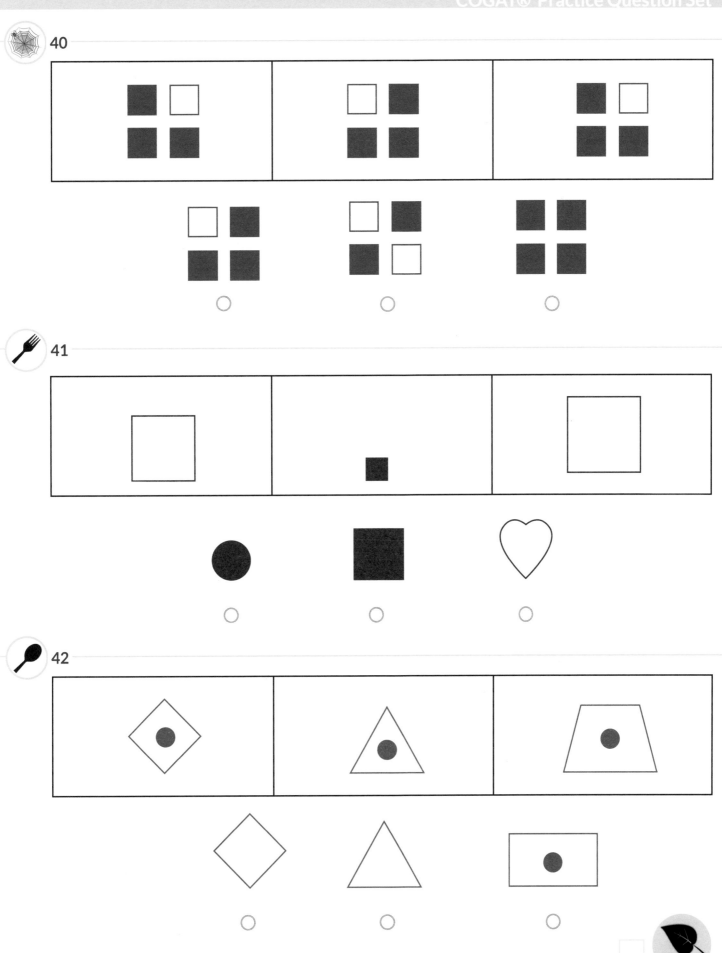

41

42

43

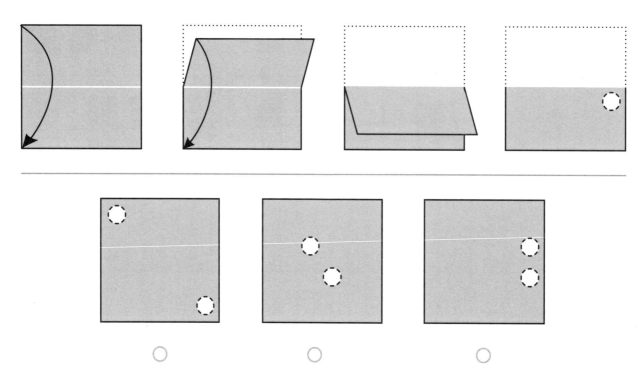

 44

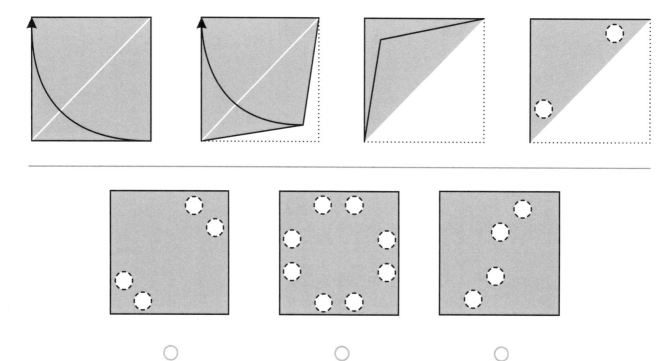

45

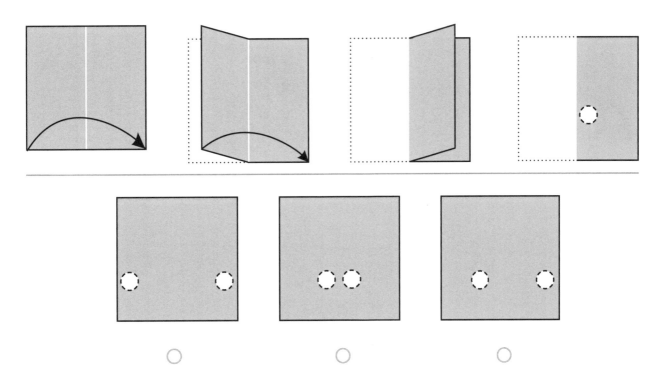

○   ○   ○

46

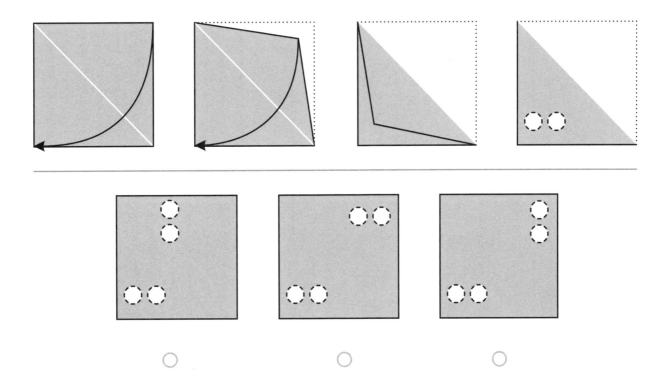

○   ○   ○

47

○ ○ ○

48

○ ○ ○

 49

○ ○ ○

50

○　　　　　　○　　　　　　○

 51

○　　　　　　○　　　　　　○

 52

○　　　　　　○　　　　　　○

1

○ ○ ○ ○

 2

○ ○ ○ ○

 3

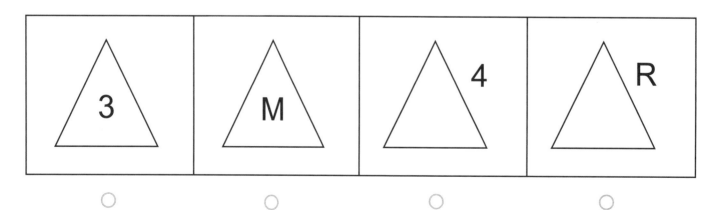

○ ○ ○ ○

4

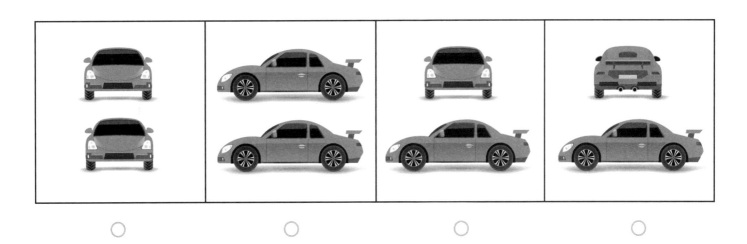

 5

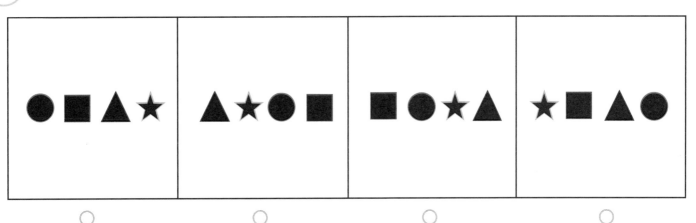

 6

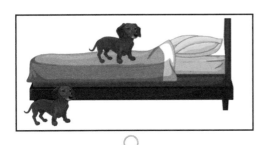

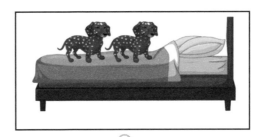

7

○   ○   ○   ○

 8

○   ○   ○   ○

 9

○   ○   ○   ○

10

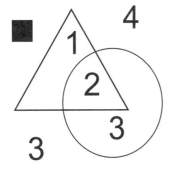

1   2      4

○   ○   ○   ○

 11

○   ○   ○   ○

12

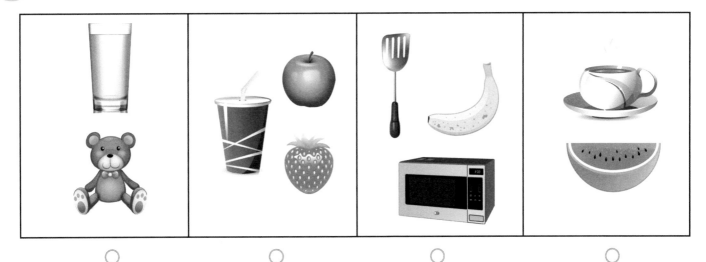

○   ○   ○   ○

13

 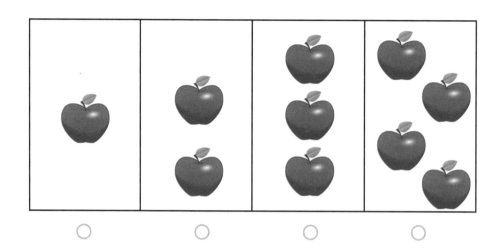

○ ○ ○ ○

 14

 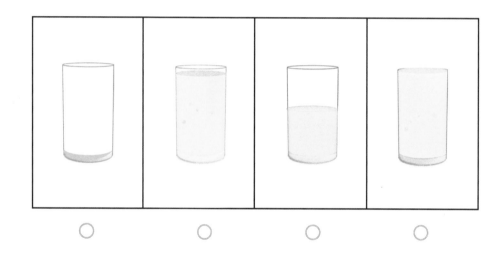

○ ○ ○ ○

 15

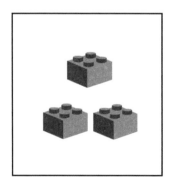 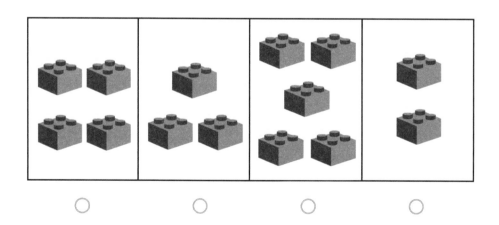

○ ○ ○ ○

16

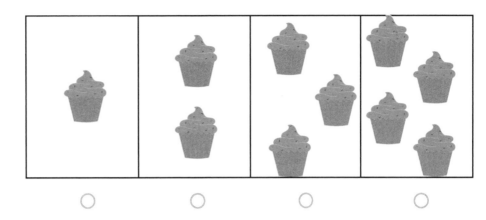

○   ○   ○   ○

 17

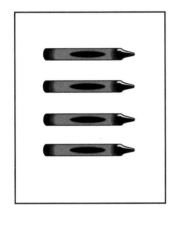 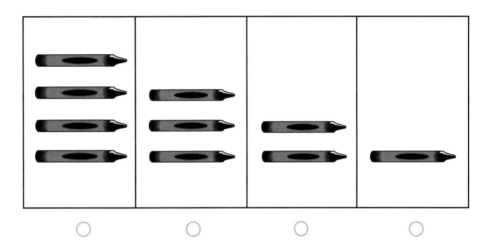

○   ○   ○   ○

 18

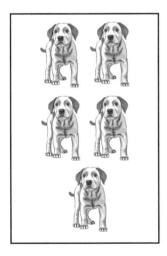 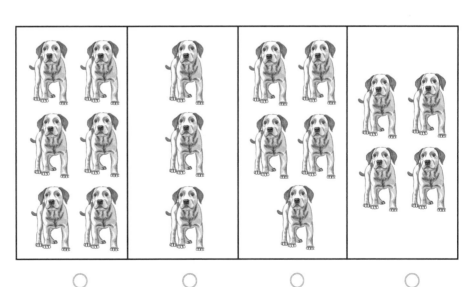

○   ○   ○   ○

19

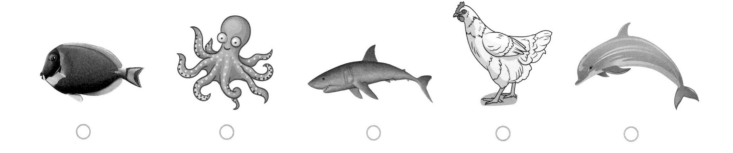

○   ○   ○   ○   ○

 20

○   ○   ○   ○   ○

 21

○   ○   ○   ○   ○

22

◯ ◯ ◯ ◯ ◯

 23

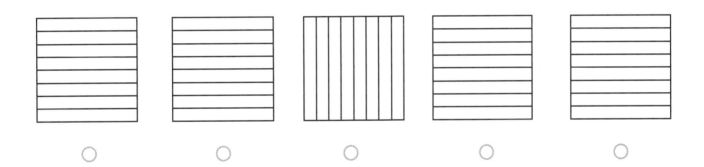

◯ ◯ ◯ ◯ ◯

 24

◯ ◯ ◯ ◯ ◯

25

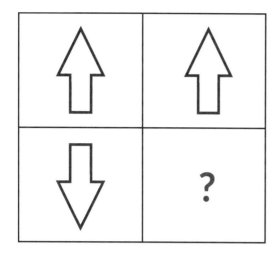    

○   ○   ○   ○

 26

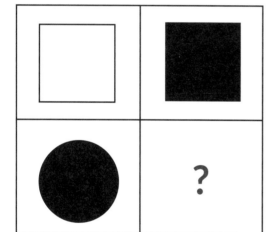 

○   ○   ○   ○

27

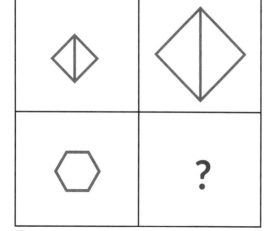   

○   ○   ○   ○

28

○   ○   ○   ○

 29

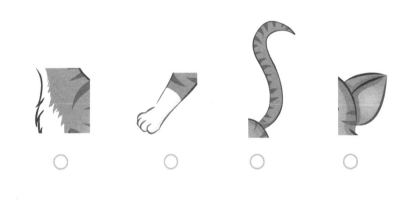

○   ○   ○   ○

 30

F	ꟻ
C	?

C   F   Ɔ   ꟻ

○   ○   ○   ○

31

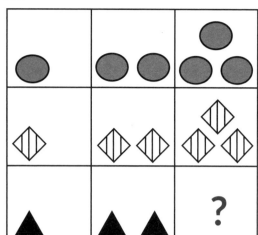 

○   ○   ○   ○

32

○   ○   ○   ○

33

○   ○   ○   ○

34

35

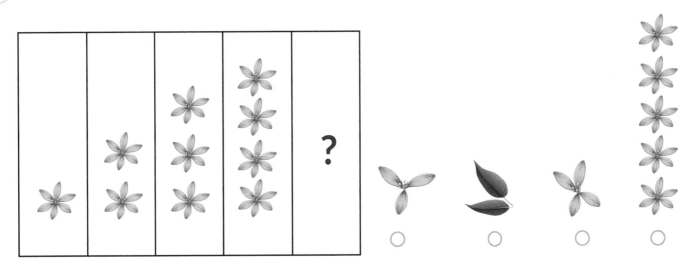

36

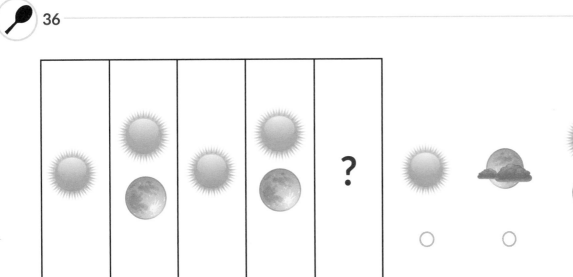

37

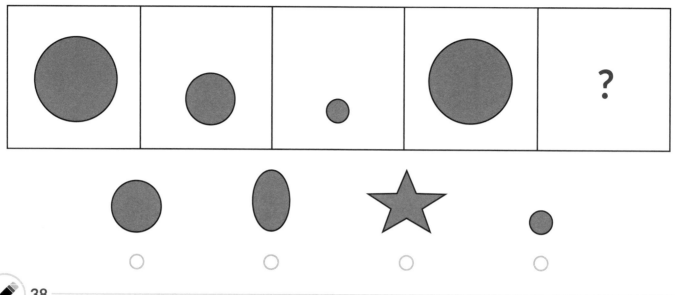

○   ○   ○   ○

38

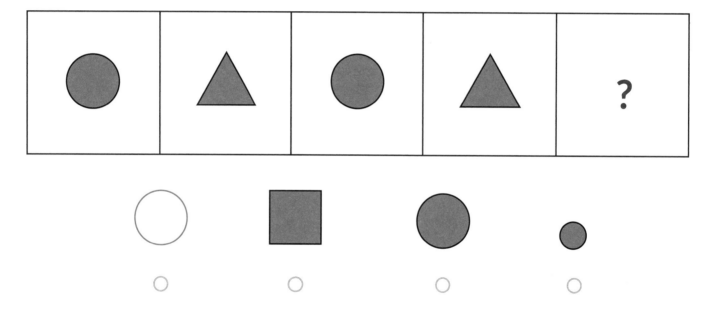

○   ○   ○   ○

Question Numbers & Answers

Identifying Similarities Using Pictures
1. B   2. C   3. C

Identifying Similarities Using Shapes/Figures
4. A   5. C (circle is inside)   6. A (triangle in middle)

Identifying Differences Using Pictures
7. D   8. C   9. C

Identifying Differences Using Shapes/Figures
10. C   11. A (circle doesn't have 4 sides)
12. D (half of shape is filled in)

Matching (The first number is the number of the picture on the top row. The second number is the number of the picture on the bottom row that it matches.)
13. 1-3; 2-5; 3-1; 4-6; 5-4; 6-2
14. 1-2; 2-3; 3-5; 4-6; 5-1; 6-4

Patterns: Picture Series
15. D   16. A   17. C   18. A

Patterns: Shape/Figure Series
19. C (circle on triangle goes: right side, bottom, left side, right side, bottom)
20. C (pattern: 1 rectangle, 1 rectangle and 1 triangle, 1 rectangle and 2 triangles, 1 rectangle, 1 rectangle and 1 triangle)
21. D (pattern: big heart, medium heart, small heart, big heart, medium heart)
22. A (pattern: one yellow block is added each time)

Picture Matrices
23. B   24. A   25. D   26. D   27. A   28. B
29. D   30. D   31. A

Shape/Figure Matrices 2x2
32. B (opposite colors)   33. D (same)
34. A (arrow in left box points same direction as arrow in right box)
35. C (another shape is added) 36. B (gets smaller)
37. C (shape is in half; blue on top and white on bottom)
38. C (the inside and outside shapes switch)
39. D (shape moves to other end of the line)
40. A (in the second box, the opposite triangles are filled in with brown)
41. A (the second shape gets smaller and is not filled in)
42. C (white shapes turn into pink shapes; pink shapes turn into white shapes)

Shape/Figure Matrices 3x3
43. C   44. B (pattern: shape points down, up, down)
45. A (pattern: shape's lines are horizontal (across), vertical (up/down), horizontal (across)
46. D (pattern: 2 shapes, 4 shapes, 6 shapes)
47. B (pattern: 1 line, 2 lines, 3 lines; horizontal (across)

Question Numbers & Answers

Shape/Figure Matrices
48. A (circle changes color from blue to yellow)
49. D (shape in the middle gets bigger)
50. B (box "flips"; and the last box "completes" the puzzle – a yellow circle on a blue square)
51. A (each row must have an oval, arrow, and star; all shapes are blue on a yellow square; the last one is missing the arrow; same is true for the columns)
52. B (the shapes change to the opposite color across the row; blue becomes yellow and yellow becomes blue)

Can You Find It?
Ocean scene 53.-55.

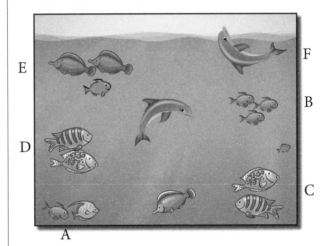

56. B   57. D   58. B   59. C   60. B   61. C   62. A
63. A   64. C   65. B   66. A   67. D   68. C

Number Series (Abacus Activity)
69. B   70. B (each rod has 1 less bead)
71. C (pattern: 1-1-2-2-3-3)
72. A (pattern: 0-3-0-2-0-1)

Number Puzzles: (Train Activity)
73. A   74. B   75. C   76. A

Number Analogies
77. C   78. B (1 is added)   79. C (3 are added)
80. A (4 are taken away)   81. C

Arithmetic Reasoning
82. B   83. B   84. D   85. D   86. C

Puzzle Completion
87. B   88. C   89. A   90. B   91. C
92. A   93. C   94. A

Paper Folding
95. C   96. B   97. C   98. B   99. A   100. C

NNAT2®/ NNAT3® PRACTICE QUESTION SET: DIRECTIONS & ANSWER KEY

Be sure to read 'Practice Question Sets Instructions' first (page 50).

Children taking the NNAT2®/ NNAT3® do not receive much verbal instruction, compared to children taking the OLSAT® and COGAT®. The directions are in the gray box. Each question type has the same directions for all the questions of that question type.

NNAT2®/ NNAT3® QUESTION TYPE 1: PATTERN COMPLETION

Directions for Pattern Completion questions (p. 51): Here is a puzzle where a piece is missing. (Point to the box that has the question mark.) Which one of the boxes in the bottom row (point to the bottom row of boxes) would go here? (Point to the box that has the question mark again.)

Question Number	Answer	Child's Answer
1	C	
2	D	
3	E	
4	C	
5	C	
6	B	
7	A	
8	E	
9	A	
10	D	

Pattern Completion Questions Answered Correctly: _____ out of 10

NNAT2®/ NNAT3® QUESTION TYPE 2: REASONING BY ANALOGY

Question Number	Answer	Child's Answer

Directions for Reasoning by Analogy questions (p. 56): Look at these pictures that are inside the boxes. One box is missing. (Point to the bottom box that has a question mark.) Now, look below at the row of answer choices. (Point to the row of answer choices.) Which one would go here? (Point to the bottom box that has a question mark again.)

Question Number	Answer
11	C (in the top row the boxes are the same; in the bottom row the boxes are the same)
12	B (in the top row the boxes are the same; in the bottom row the boxes are the same)
13	A (in each row: one arrow points up, one arrow points to side)
14	D (same)
15	B (opposite)
16	D (blue turns to yellow, yellow turns to blue)
17	A (one shape is added)
18	A (the lines point: down, up, down)
19	D (whole shape, half shape, whole shape)
20	A (half blue, other half yellow, blue half+yellow half together)
21	B (each row has one of each: up arrow, heart, star)
22	D (yellow shape; larger blue shape; yellow shape inside blue shape)

Reasoning by Analogy Questions Answered Correctly: _____ out of 12

COGAT® PRACTICE QUESTION SET: DIRECTIONS & ANSWER KEY

Be sure to read 'Practice Question Sets Instructions' first (page 50).

This answer key is divided into charts according to COGAT® question type so that you can easily see how your child performs on each of the test's nine question types. Each chart includes the directions you will read to your child. It also lists the page navigation icons and question navigation icons that you will read to your child to assist with navigation.

1) If turning to a new page, say to your child: "Find the page where there is a(n) ___ at the bottom." (These sentences are listed in each chart in *italics*.)
2) Next, say to your child: "Find the row where there is a(n) ___. " (These are the question navigation icons listed in the first column. They are <u>underlined</u>.)
3) Then, read the directions to your child. These are in the gray box. Each question type has the same directions for the questions of that question type. (The directions are the same for all questions of the same question type.) The only exception is the last question type on p. 98 (Sentence Completion). In the Sentence Completion chart, the directions are in the chart's third column and not in a gray box.

COGAT® QUESTION TYPE 1: PICTURE ANALOGIES

Directions for all Picture Analogy questions: Look at these boxes that are on top. The pictures that are inside belong together in some way. Then, look at these boxes that are on the bottom. One of these boxes on the bottom is empty. Look next to the boxes. There is a row of pictures. Which one would go together with this picture that is in the bottom box like these pictures that are in the top boxes?

"Find the row where there is a(n) _____."	Question Number	Answer	Child's Answer
(p. 62) *"Find the page where there is an umbrella at the bottom."* (Help child find the page where questions start.)			
<u>star</u>	1	B	
<u>fish</u>	2	C	
<u>chair</u>	3	B	
(p. 63) *"Find the page where there is a ball at the bottom."*			
<u>car</u>	4	B	
<u>cup</u>	5	A	
<u>duck</u>	6	B	

Picture Analogy Questions Answered Correctly: _____ out of 6

COGAT® QUESTION TYPE 2: PICTURE CLASSIFICATION

Directions for all Picture Classification questions: Look at the top row of pictures. These pictures are alike in a certain way. Then, look at the pictures that are on the bottom row. Which picture that is in the bottom row would go best with the pictures that are in the top row?

"Find the row where there is a(n) _____."	Question Number	Answer	Child's Answer
(p. 64) *"Find the page where there is a house at the bottom."*			
<u>shirt</u>	7	C	
<u>truck</u>	8	B	
<u>crab</u>	9	A	
(p. 65) *"Find the page where there is a pair of glasses at the bottom."*			
<u>spider web</u>	10	C	
<u>fork</u>	11	B	
<u>spoon</u>	12	A	

Picture Classification Questions Answered Correctly: _____ out of 6

COGAT® QUESTION TYPE 3: NUMBER SERIES (ABACUS)

Directions for all Number Series questions: Here's an abacus. The "circles" on the abacus are beads. These beads are on rods. The beads on the first five rods have made a pattern. Look at the last rod on the abacus. The beads on this rod are missing. Next to the abacus are three rods. These are the answer choices. Choose which rod would go in the place of the last rod in order to complete the pattern.

"Find the row where there is a(n) _____."	Question Number	Answer	Child's Answer
(p. 66) *"Find the page where there is an eye at the bottom."*			
star	13	C (1-3-1-3)	
cup	14	C (1 bead gets added)	
chair	15	A (5-3-1)	
(p. 67) *"Find the page where there is a bike at the bottom."*			
car	16	C (0-1-3)	
fish	17	C (1 bead gets taken away)	
shirt	18	B (2-2-2-3-3-3)	

Number Series Questions Answered Correctly: _____ out of 6

COGAT® QUESTION TYPE 4: MATH PUZZLES (TRAIN)

Directions for all Math Puzzles questions: Look at the trains on the top and bottom. They have things inside. These two trains must have the same number of things. You need to put a train car in place of the train car that has a question mark so that the second train has the same number of things as the other train. Which train car should you choose so that the second train has the same number of things as the first train?

"Find the row where there is a(n) _____."	Question Number	Answer	Child's Answer
(p. 68) *"Find the page where there is a table at the bottom."*			
pencil	19	A	
star	20	B	
crab	21	C	
(p. 69) *"Find the page where there is a hand at the bottom."*			
spider web	22	B	
fork	23	C	
spoon	24	B	

Math Puzzles Questions Answered Correctly: _____ out of 6

COGAT® QUESTION TYPE 5: NUMBER ANALOGIES

Directions for all Number Analogy questions: Look at these boxes that are on top. The pictures that are inside belong together in some way. Then, look at these boxes that are on the bottom. One of these boxes on the bottom is empty. Look next to the boxes. There is a row of pictures. Which one would go together with this picture that is in the bottom box like these pictures that are in the top boxes?

"Find the row where there is a(n) _____."	Question Number	Answer	Child's Answer
(p. 70) *"Find the page where there is a butterfly at the bottom."*			
cup	25	C (+3)	
triangle	26	A (same)	
duck	27	B (-5)	
(p. 71) *"Find the page where there is a boot at the bottom."*			
key	28	B (half)	
truck	29	A (double)	
bug	30	C (half)	

Number Analogies Questions Answered Correctly: _____ out of 6

COGAT® QUESTION TYPE 6: FIGURE MATRICES

Directions for all Figure Matrices questions: Look at these boxes that are on top. The pictures that are inside belong together in some way. Then, look at these boxes that are on the bottom. One of these boxes on the bottom is empty. Look next to the boxes. There is a row of pictures. Which one would go together with this picture that is in the bottom box like these pictures that are in the top boxes?

"Find the row where there is a(n) _____."	Question Number	Answer	Child's Answer
(p. 72) *"Find the page where there is a train at the bottom."*			
ant	31	A (same)	
cup	32	C (makes pattern)	
chair	33	A (one shape is added)	
(p. 73) *"Find the page where there is a bird at the bottom."*			
car	34	C (turns to face other way)	
fish	35	B (vertical lines added)	
shirt	36	C (gets flipped)	

Figure Matrices Questions Answered Correctly: _____ out of 6

COGAT® QUESTION TYPE 7: FIGURE CLASSIFICATION

Directions for all Figure Classification questions: Look at the top row of pictures. These pictures are alike in a certain way. Then, look at the pictures that are on the bottom row. Which picture that is in the bottom row would go best with the pictures that are in the top row?

"Find the row where there is a(n) _____."	Question Number	Answer	Child's Answer
(p. 74) *"Find the page where there is ice cream at the bottom."*			
duck	37	C	
truck	38	B	
crab	39	B (triangle & square must be opposite colors)	
(p. 75) *"Find the page where there is a leaf at the bottom."*			
spider web	40	A (3 squares must be pink)	
fork	41	B (must be square)	
spoon	42	C (must have circle inside)	

Figure Classification Questions Answered Correctly: _____ out of 6

COGAT® QUESTION TYPE 8: PAPER FOLDING

Directions for all Paper Folding questions: Look at the top row of pictures. These show a sheet of paper, how it was folded, and how holes were made in the folded sheet of paper. Look at these pictures that are on the bottom row. Which picture shows how the paper would look after the paper is unfolded?

"Find the row where there is a(n) _____."	Question Number	Answer	Child's Answer
(p. 76) *"Find the page where there is a stoplight at the bottom."*			
cup	43	C	
chair	44	A	
(p. 77) *"Find the page where there is a boat at the bottom."*			
fish	45	B	
shirt	46	C	

Paper Folding Questions Answered Correctly: _____ out of 4

COGAT® QUESTION TYPE 9: SENTENCE COMPLETION

"Find the row where there is a(n)___."	Question Number	Directions (Say to child)	Answer	Child's Answer
(p. 78) *"Find the page where there is a shoe at the bottom."*				
arrow	47	Which one would live in a river?	C	
triangle	48	Which one would you see in a kitchen?	B	
key	49	Which one would you use with paper?	C	
(p. 79) *"Find the page where there is a flower at the bottom."*				
pencil	50	Which one is not picked from a tree?	A	
bug	51	Which one is not an instrument?	C	
star	52	Which one would fly?	B	

Sentence Completion Questions Answered Correctly: _____ out of 6

OLSAT® PRACTICE QUESTION SET: DIRECTIONS & ANSWER KEY

Be sure to read 'Practice Question Sets Instructions' first (page 50).

This answer key is divided into charts according to OLSAT® question type so that you can easily see how your child performs in each of the test's 10 sections.

Each chart includes the directions you will read to your child. It also lists the page marker icons and question marker icons that you will read to your child to assist with navigation.

1) If turning to a new page, say to your child: "Find the page where there is a(n) ___ at the bottom." (These sentences are listed in each chart in *italics*.)
2) Next, say to your child: "Find the row where there is a(n) ___. " (These are the question navigation icons listed in the first column. These are underlined.)
3) Then, read the directions to your child. These are in the chart's third column. *For the last seven question types (p.100-101) the directions are in the gray box above that question type's chart. These last question types have the same directions for all the questions of that question type. (The directions are repeated.)

OLSAT® QUESTION TYPE 1: FOLLOWING DIRECTIONS

"Find the row where there is a(n) ___."	Question Number	Directions (Say to child)	Answer	Child's Answer
(p. 80) *"Find the page where there is an umbrella at the bottom."*				
star	1	Which picture shows a monkey upside down under a tree?	D	
fish	2	These pictures are out of order. Which picture would be first?	C	
chair	3	Which picture shows a number inside a triangle?	A	
(p.81) *"Find the page where there is a soccer ball at the bottom."*				
duck	4	Which picture shows both cars sideways?	B	
cup	5	Which picture shows the shapes like this: a circle is in the middle, a triangle is last, and a square is first?	C	
shirt	6	Which picture shows two dogs that are exactly the same and standing on top of the bed?	D	

Following Directions Questions Answered Correctly: _____ out of 6

OLSAT® QUESTION TYPE 2: AURAL REASONING

"Find the row where there is a(n) ___."	Question Number	Directions (Say to child)	Answer	Child's Answer
(p. 82) *"Find the page where there is a house at the bottom."*				
spoon	7	Which picture shows two pairs of the same flower?	B	
truck	8	Which picture shows one animal that lives in water and two animals that live on land?	D	
fork	9	Which one would a farmer use?	B	
(p. 83) *"Find the page where there is a pair of glasses at the bottom."*				
spider web	10	Look at the picture on the left. (Point to the picture on the left.) Then, look at these pictures on the right. (Point to the row of answer choices.) Which one shows the number that is inside neither the circle nor the triangle?	D	
crab	11	Which thing would you find at a library?	A	
car	12	Which picture shows one thing you would drink and two things you would eat?	B	

Aural Reasoning Questions Answered Correctly: _____ out of 6

OLSAT® QUESTION TYPE 3: ARITHMETIC REASONING

"Find the row where there is a(n) ___."	Question Number	Directions (Say to child)	Answer	Child's Answer
(p. 84) *"Find the page where there is an eye at the bottom."*				
star	13	Alex has the number of apples that is in the box at the beginning of the row. Katie has twice as many apples as Alex has. Which box shows how many apples Katie has?	D	
cup	14	Sophie has the amount of water in the glass that is in the box at the beginning of the row. She pours half of her water out of the glass. Which box shows how much water is left in the glass?	C	
chair	15	Tommy has the number of blocks that is in the box at the beginning of the row. Tommy has more blocks than Brian has. Which box shows the number of blocks Brian has?	D	
(p. 85) *"Find the page where there is a bike at the bottom."*				
car	16	There are 5 people coming to Kelly's party. Kelly needs to make 1 cupcake for each person coming to her party. In the box at the beginning of the row is the number of cupcakes Kelly has made. Which box shows how many more cupcakes Kelly needs to make?	C	
fish	17	Lee has the number of crayons that is in the box at the beginning of the row. Maria has the same number of crayons. Which box shows how many crayons Maria has?	A	
shirt	18	Shelly has the number of puppies that is in the box at the beginning of the row. Shelly gives away 2 puppies to her friends. Which box shows how many puppies Shelly has now?	B	

Arithmetic Reasoning Questions Answered Correctly: _____ out of 6

OLSAT® QUESTION TYPE 4: PICTURE CLASSIFICATION

Directions for all Picture Classification questions: Look at this row of pictures. One of these pictures in the row does not belong. This picture is not like the others in the row. Which picture does not belong?

"Find the row where there is a(n) ___."	Question Number	Answer	Child's Answer
(p. 86) *"Find the page where there is a table at the bottom."*			
pencil	19	D	
star	20	C	
crab	21	C	
(p. 87) *"Find the page where there is a hand at the bottom."*			
spider web	22	D	

Picture Classification Questions Answered Correctly: _____ out of 4

OLSAT® QUESTION TYPE 5: FIGURE CLASSIFICATION

Directions for all Figure Classification questions: Look at this row of pictures. One of these pictures in the row does not belong. This picture is not like the others in the row. Which picture does not belong?

"Find the row where there is a(n) ___."	Question Number	Answer	Child's Answer
fork	23	C (inside lines going a different way)	
spoon	24	A (different shape in the middle)	

Figure Classification Questions Answered Correctly: _____ out of 2

OLSAT® QUESTION TYPE 6: FIGURE ANALOGIES

Directions for all Figure Analogy questions: Look at these boxes that are on top. The pictures that are inside belong together in some way. Then, look at these boxes that are on the bottom. One of these boxes on the bottom is empty. Look next to the boxes. There is a row of pictures. Which one would go together with this picture that is in the bottom box like these pictures that are in the top boxes?

"Find the row where there is a(n) ___."	Question Number	Answer	Child's Answer
(p. 88) *"Find the page where there is a train at the bottom."*			
ant	25	B (same arrow, pointing same way)	
cup	26	B (black becomes white; white becomes black)	
chair	27	D (gets bigger)	

Figure Analogies Questions Answered Correctly: _____ out of 3

OLSAT® QUESTION TYPE 7: PICTURE ANALOGIES

Directions for all Picture Analogy questions: Look at these boxes that are on top. The pictures that are inside belong together in some way. Then, look at these boxes that are on the bottom. One of these boxes on the bottom is empty. Look next to the boxes. There is a row of pictures. Which one would go together with this picture that is in the bottom box like these pictures that are in the top boxes?

"Find the row where there is a(n)___."	Question Number	Answer	Child's Answer
(p. 89) *"Find the page where there is a bird at the bottom."*			
car	28	B	
fish	29	D	
shirt	30	C (letter flipped backwards)	

Picture Analogies Questions Answered Correctly: _____ out of 3

OLSAT® QUESTION TYPE 8: PATTERN MATRIX

Directions for all Pattern Matrix questions: Look at these pictures that are inside the boxes. Look at the last box. It is empty. Beside the boxes there is a row of pictures. Which one should go inside the empty box that is in the bottom row?

"Find the row where there is a(n)___."	Question Number	Answer	Child's Answer
(p. 90) *"Find the page where there is ice cream at the bottom."*			
duck	31	A (across the rows, one shape is added each time)	
truck	32	D (pattern across:2 shapes-1 shape-2 shapes) (same shape)	
crab	33	C (1 line-2 lines-1 line; same line type)	

Pattern Matrix Questions Answered Correctly: _____ out of 3

OLSAT® QUESTION TYPE 9: PICTURE SERIES

Directions for all Picture Series questions: Look at this row of boxes. The pictures that are inside belong together in some way. Another picture should go inside the empty box. Next to the boxes there is a row of pictures. Which one should go inside the empty box?

"Find the row where there is a(n) ___."	Question Number	Answer	Child's Answer
(p. 91) *"Find the page where there is a leaf at the bottom."*			
spider web	34	A	
fork	35	D	
spoon	36	A	

Picture Series Questions Answered Correctly: _____ out of 3

OLSAT® QUESTION TYPE 10: FIGURE SERIES

Directions for all Figure Series questions: Look at this row of boxes. The pictures that are inside belong together in some way. Another picture should go inside the empty box. Under the boxes there is a row of pictures. Which one should go inside the empty box?

"Find the row where there is a(n) ___."	Question Number	Answer	Child's Answer
(p. 92) *"Find the page where there is a shoe at the bottom."*			
bug	37	A (large-medium-small-large-medium)	
pencil	38	C	

Figure Series Questions Answered Correctly: _____ out of 2

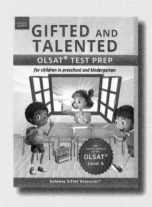 
Did your child finish the exercises? Here's a certificate for your new detective! (Please cut along the dotted lines.)

The Gifted Detective Agency

Congratulations to:

_____

Our Newest Member!